M000316497

Endorsements

Powerful! What's the sound of a jaw hitting the floor? How do I get everybody I know to read this book? *Approaching Armageddon* proves the validity of the Bible—beyond a shadow of a doubt—like no book I've ever read. You won't want to put it down. Best book of the year, if you ask me. Bible prophecy books are sometimes speculative and unconvincing, but *Approaching Armageddon* stands apart. Air-tight Bible teaching that will convince even the skeptic of Jesus' soon coming.

Scott Ritsema
Author, Producer of "Media on the Brain"
Speaker/Director of Belt of Truth Ministries

Steve Wohlberg has done it again! He has taken the complex and broken it down for everyone to understand. *Approaching Armageddon* is timely, biblical, and interesting. It is refreshing to read a book that wades into so many challenging subjects with simplicity and sanctified logic. This Christ-centered approach to the subject of last-day events, especially the signs that portend the soon coming "Battle of Armageddon," is worthy of wide circulation. May it be instrumental in waking many Christians up and leading countless more to a saving relationship with, as Steve calls Him, "the Prophecy Man."

Allen Barnes
Director of Plain People Ministries

I was very excited when I saw another book coming out from Steve Wohlberg. What a timely topic, too! With Steve's deep understanding of Bible prophecy and his God-given ability to explain it so the average lay person can also understand it, this is definitely a must-read. With our world seemingly spinning out of control, this book can definitely give hope just when we need it most.

Kevin Bryant, MD

With his eyes on both the Bible and today's headlines, Steve Wohlberg perfectly articulates how biblical prophecy is now playing out before our very eyes in current world events. *Approaching Armageddon* reveals the truth about the chaos that surrounds us and opens eyes and hearts to the hope that we have in Christ Jesus, while strengthening our faith and preparing us to confidently give answers to all those who are lost, fearful, and confused.

Rob Pue
Publisher, Wisconsin Christian News
Commentator, VCY America Radio Network
Host of WCN-TV

Approaching Armageddon is a striking wake-up call for planet earth. Steve has clearly identified many end-time signs and proven how these signs are a direct fulfillment of Bible prophecy. Most importantly, he reveals how we can stand victorious in these final days! I highly recommend this book to anyone who desires to understand the perilous days we are living in and be prepared for the soon return of Jesus!

Dustin Pestlin
President, Hope Through Prophecy

Are the unprecedented number and magnitude of frightening world events merely random and chaotic happenings? Or a long-foretold and long-awaited signal? Clear, fascinating, and gripping, *Approaching Armageddon* is a must-read!

Subodh K. Pandit, MD
Author of *Does God Really Exist?* and *Setting the Record Straight on Atheism, Agnosticism and Evolution*
Speaker of the video series, "God Fact or Fiction?"
www.searchseminars.org

Approaching Armageddon is a must-read. Just as science has rules that guide careful scientists, Bible prophecies have rules that guide careful biblical scholars. In his gripping and easy reading style, Steve Wohlberg has managed to untangle important endgame prophecies using long-validated rules of good prophetic interpretation. He leads you on a compelling journey into the prophecies letting the Bible explain its own symbols. If you desire conspiracy theories, hype, and sensational nonsense that seems to plague books of this genre, you'll be disappointed in this book. But if you seek to understand the Bible's end-time prophecies, you will be as delighted with this book as I was.

Phil Mills, MD

In this time of uncertainty, when the world appears to be turning upside-down, there is anxiety and depression everywhere. People are confused and are afraid to trust the news, the government, and everyone in general. This is the perfect time for Steve Wohlberg's latest book, *Approaching Armageddon,* to be published. It is an easy-to-read, gripping, excellent, sweeping biblical summary of the prophecies of the last days of this earth's history. Instead of causing fear, however, it provides Bible answers to give us a calm, abiding trust in Jesus as our Savior. It will inspire you to more carefully read and study your Bible and find Jesus at the very center of the last book of the Bible. This gem is a must-read.

Ron Fleck, MD
President, Second Hope Ministries International

Once again Steve Wohlberg has written an engaging and compelling book that is a great wake-up call to all of us. Steve gives us hope in the midst of the troubles this world is going through.

Jeff Zaremsky
Director of *Shalom Adventure* magazine
www.ShalomAdventure.com

APPROACHING ARMAGEDDON

DISCOVER HOPE
BEYOND EARTH'S
FINAL BATTLE

APPROACHING ARMAGEDDON

STEVE WOHLBERG

DESTINY IMAGE® PUBLISHERS, INC.
P.O. Box 310, Shippensburg, PA 17257-0310
"Promoting Inspired Lives."

This book and all other Destiny Image and Destiny Image Fiction books are available at Christian bookstores and distributors worldwide.

Cover design by: Jaime Galvez and Eileen Rockwell

For more information on foreign distributors, call 717-532-3040.

Reach us on the Internet: www.destinyimage.com.

ISBN 13 TP: 978-0-7684-5807-7

ISBN 13 eBook: 978-0-7684-5808-4

For Worldwide Distribution, Printed in the U.S.A.

1 2 3 4 5 6 7 8 / 25 24 23 22 21 20

SPECIAL THANKS

To Don Nori, Jr., CEO of the
Nori Media Group / Destiny Image Publishers,
for believing in this project.

To your team that was able to bring this book
from manuscript to publication in
record time. Great job!

To Tim Saxton, who helped me with
critical research for this manuscript.

To all of my friends at White Horse Media.
It is wonderful to work with each of you!

To my wife Kristin, Seth, and Abby,
for your love and patience with Dad.

Above all, to my Creator who always fulfills His
promises, such as "Fear not, I will help you"
(see Isa. 43:1-3).

CONTENTS

FOREWORD

I guess it was about twenty years ago now that I had a "divine appointment" with my television set. It was one of those rare nights when, no matter what I did, I was not able to fall asleep. So I got up and read from the Scriptures, prayed, and went back to bed. As the minutes ticked by on the clock on my bedside table, sleep still eluded me.

Frustrated, I went to the living room and turned on my favorite Christian TV channel. It was late at night, and there was a program on that I had not seen before. Here was a Bible teacher explaining the end times and Bible prophecy. Now, I had studied Bible prophecy for years; I had read Daniel, Revelation, Thessalonians, and, in fact, the *whole* Bible multiple times in depth, but after so many years of study, I still was unable to make a conclusive, comfortable connection between what I read in my Bible and what 99 percent of pastors and prophecy writers were saying.

It was as if they had to twist and contort Scripture, take things out of context and move them around in space and time in order to fit *their* narrative. And it just never made sense. Why would one have to make such enormous leaps of faith and blindly accept the teaching and counsel of men in order for God's Word to line up with popular end-times theology? God doesn't hide His truths from us. The Scriptures still exist today, thousands of years after they were given by inspiration of God, for *our* benefit. James 1:5 offers the promise, *"If any of you lacks wisdom, let him ask of God, who gives to all liberally and without reproach, and it will be given to him."*

I had been seeking clear answers that lined up with the Bible clearly, easily, perfectly, without being *forced*, like a square peg in a round hole, to fit a preconceived narrative—a narrative that was very, very popular and being taught from nearly every pulpit in the evangelical world.

At first, I watched this teacher on the television with a bit of skepticism—I had seen so many before and they were all saying the exact same thing. But this night was different. Here was a Bible teacher explaining prophecy in a way that I had never seen or heard before and backing up everything he was teaching with God's Word. He was not twisting or contorting Scripture or asking people to make assumptions, take giant leaps of faith, or take his word for it. Instead, he was *showing* us in God's Word exactly what God had said and explaining things in a way that finally, for the first time in my life, made sense. His conclusions were practical, reasonable, and logical. And as I watched, a veil was lifted from my eyes. I was finally able to understand those "confusing" books of the Bible in a way that made perfect sense. Here was a Bible teacher who took God's Word literally and explained the "hard things" so clearly that anyone could easily understand them.

That teacher was Steve Wohlberg.

I couldn't wait to share what I was learning with my wife and many others. We continued to watch the entire series of presentations from Steve. I later purchased several of his books and video teachings. We even held small group meetings to share the video lessons with others. Many eyes were opened.

Some time later, a friend, knowing I had been studying Steve's work, suggested I get in touch with him and invite him to write a monthly column in the Christian newspaper I publish. This friend gave me Steve's phone number and I called—wondering if this "famous TV preacher" would even be willing to speak to a "little fish" like me. I was pleasantly surprised to find Steve not only warm and cordial, but friendly and excited to become one of our regular columnists. And his monthly articles ran in our newspaper every month for over a decade, reaching countless thousands of readers whose eyes were also opened to the simple, plain truths of God's Word regarding end-times prophecy and much more.

Steve has since authored more books than I can count, on a wide variety of topics—topics that are of vital importance for a biblical understanding of the times we're living in. In addition to Bible prophecy, he's written on witchcraft, the occult, "new age" religions, death and the life to come for believers in Christ, the "emergent" church and the great falling away, natural health issues, and much more.

Steve is not afraid to blow the trumpet of warning regarding "sensitive" topics that many pastors refuse to ever preach on. But even as he exposes the wicked deeds of darkness, he does so, every time, with a message of *hope*. The blessed hope that we can all be assured of as Christ-followers.

The book you're about to read is as relevant as today's newspaper headlines. Thank you for buying a copy. If you've never read any of Steve's work before, you're in for a real treat. I am confident you'll find the teaching eye-opening and captivating, a "page-turner" if you will, as you discover the answers you've been seeking regarding all that is taking place in our world *right now*. You may find parts of the book that will challenge your theology. But let me ask you this: if what you *thought* you knew about your theology was wrong, *when* would you want to know?

The time is now, friends. Just as God Himself closed the door of the Ark and only a small remnant was saved, there is coming soon that great and terrible Day of the Lord, and then there will be no second chances.

But *Approaching Armageddon* isn't just for you. It's meant to equip you to go and make disciples, teaching them to obey all Jesus commanded. Soon—I believe very soon—the lost souls around us will be looking to *us* for answers. And in a world of lies, they'll be desperate for the truth. Are you ready to give those answers? Are you confident in your biblical knowledge and understanding? I hope you are, because *you* have been called into the Great Commission in these closing days of planet Earth and there are souls out there starving for God's truth, and it's up to you to feed and care for these lost, confused sheep. Don't take your commission lightly.

This book will equip you and give you the confidence you need to provide those answers in a clear and understandable way. And as we know from 1 Peter 3:15, we must *"Always be prepared to give an answer to everyone who asks you to give the reason for the hope that you have."* Amen.

Approaching Armageddon is, at once, a warning, a clear explanation, and a message of hope for all who will come to Christ in repentance and faith. Indeed, it is a vital message with *eternal* significance!

Rob Pue
Publisher, Wisconsin Christian News
Commentator, VCY America Radio Network
Host, WCN-TV

INTRODUCTION

What's going on? millions wonder as they witness chaotic events that keep rattling planet Earth. The steady disintegration of family values, deadly diseases like the novel coronavirus, economic upheavals, unprecedented hostilities between political parties, explosive racial tensions, protests and riots, LGBTQ controversies, rising depression and suicide rates, plus countless other shock waves keep ripping humans apart.

Even nature itself seems to have gone berserk. Record heat waves, decimating cold spells, rising sea levels, food shortages, and mass animal die-offs are all being discussed on CNN, Fox News, throughout social media, and on news apps. If that isn't enough, killer earthquakes, monster storms, fierce wildfires, destructive tsunamis, raging floods, and lava-spewing volcanoes just keep pounding humanity—with no end in sight.

People's heads are spinning.

By the time you read this, new woes will undoubtedly have smitten too many of us.

What's next? millions anxiously inquire.

Is there any possible way to make sense out of such apparent senselessness? Are we human beings nothing more than fragile life forms on a planet twirling randomly through mindless space toward our eventual demise, without any firm hope of a happy, permanent future?

Personally, I don't believe that dismal scenario for a minute. It's true that life on earth is getting tougher, but rest assured that *Approaching Armageddon* isn't only about Bad News. Definitely not! There's Good News, too. In fact, a big picture exists that is sensible and offers hope for everyone—whatever our skin color, physical ailments, past failures, or the size of our bank accounts. Believe it or not (and I'll offer solid evidence shortly), this larger perspective has been accurately revealed in the pages of an ancient book—the Holy Bible.

In the following pages, I'm going to highlight numerous easy-to-grasp biblical signs—like road signs on a highway—indicative that earth's present chaos is entirely symptomatic of the fact that humanity has entered a unique period of history called *"the time of the end"* (Dan. 12:4). I'll also explain what's on the ultimate horizon—beyond Armageddon—which is unimaginably glorious to those who choose to be part of it.

But before this book examines those signs, I will offer sensible reasons why—in the midst of widespread skepticism, agnosticism, and atheism—we *can* have confidence that ancient biblical predictions are both trustworthy and accurate and not simply the fare of sensationalist tabloids.

"Come now, and let us reason together," wrote the prophet Isaiah (Isa. 1:18). It is my sincere hope and prayer that as you ponder the sobering information within these pages you will discover a God of infinite love, enthroned above earth's chaos, and a bright tomorrow.

"Let not your heart be troubled," declared the greatest Teacher this world has ever seen (John 14:1).

"Peace I leave with you," is His promise (John 14:27).

We all need His peace today.

CHAPTER 1

THE PROPHECY MAN

> **"Wise men still seek Him."**
>
> —Popular saying on bumper stickers, magnets,
> decals, Christmas tree ornaments

Before I explain what "The Prophecy Man" is all about, here's a quick quiz question: Can you guess what book is the world's all-time bestselling volume? It has been printed by more printing presses, translated into more languages, and purchased in more countries than any other book ever written in the history of literature.

No, it's not *Harry Potter*, but the Holy Bible.

That, in itself, should cause us to candidly consider its contents. Yes, of course, I realize that skeptics abound who don't believe that the Bible is an inspired book; but honestly, such skepticism isn't new.

The ideas of the French atheist Voltaire (1694–1778) greatly contributed to the infamous French Revolution (1793–1797), during which the French legislative assembly literally burned Bibles and abolished religion. "It took 12 men to originate the Christian religion," Voltaire famously declared, "but it will take but one to eliminate it. Within fifty years from now the only Bible will be in museums."

Voltaire was wrong.

He's dead—but the Bible lives on.

Not only that, but the French Revolution, which was influenced by Voltaire's teachings, became so horrific and disastrous that shortly after rivers of blood flowed through the streets of Paris, France's same legislative assembly that abolished Christianity reversed course, giving both the Bible and belief in God legal protection. A few years later, the Geneva Bible Society purchased Voltaire's house in Paris and turned it into its home base to print stacks of Bibles!

"The Bible is an anvil that has worn out many a hammer" is an old saying that still rings true today.

Here's another quiz question: Can you guess the name of history's most famous Person? More books have been written about Him *by far* than about any other human being who has ever walked this earth. Not only that, but this unique Person has more followers today worldwide than any other religious leader who has ever taught among men, including Moses, Mohammed, Buddha, or Confucius *combined*. It's the truth. That Person is Jesus, also called the Christ. The Holy Bible calls Him the "Prince of Peace" (Isa. 9:6). Today His religion, Christianity—in spite of the failures of many of His professed followers—*is the largest religion in the world*.

What makes Jesus Christ unique above all other humans? Many things, but perhaps His most astonishing feature are the numerous *prophecies* pinpointing His birthplace, hometown, teachings, betrayal, suffering, and manner of death that He uniquely *fulfilled*. Honestly, *no other religion* can make such claims about its founder or about anyone else for that matter. Wicca has nothing like this in its magical teachings. Neither does Islam, Hinduism, or Buddhism. It's a fact—there simply aren't any prophecies in the Koran, Hindu writings, Buddhist works, or in the New Age movement predicting definite events in advance that have literally been fulfilled in real history. But the Bible has lots of these prophecies, and many were uniquely fulfilled by Jesus. The details are astounding. Here are only a few examples.

Over 700 years before Jesus was born, the prophet Isaiah predicted:

*The Lord Himself will give you a sign: Behold, **the virgin shall conceive and bear a Son**, and shall call His name Immanuel* [meaning, "God is with us"] (Isaiah 7:14).

While many have always found the idea that Jesus was conceived inside of a virgin woman hard to believe, this is exactly what the New Testament describes. The book of Luke reports:

*Now in the sixth month the angel Gabriel was sent by God to a city of Galilee named Nazareth, **to a virgin** betrothed to a man whose name was Joseph, of the house of David. **The virgin's name was Mary**. And having come in, the angel said to her, "Rejoice, highly favored one, the Lord is with you; blessed are you among women!" But when she saw him, she was troubled at his saying, and considered what manner of greeting this was. Then the angel said to her, "Do not be afraid, Mary, for you have found favor with God. And behold, you will conceive in your womb and bring forth a Son, and shall call His name Jesus. He will be great, and will be called the Son of the Highest; and the Lord God will give Him the throne*

of His father David. And He will reign over the house
of Jacob forever, and of His kingdom there will be no
end" (Luke 1:26-33).

According to the biblical record, Jesus was miraculously conceived deep within the womb of His mother
(Mary) *before she had physical intimacy with any man.*
Thus, *Jesus had no earthy father.* His conception was
wholly supernatural.

After hearing these astonishing words from the lips of
a holy angel, Mary blurted out, *"How can this be, since I do*
not know a man?" (Luke 1:34). Good question, Mary! *How*
can this be? Notice carefully:

And the angel answered and said to her, "The Holy
Spirit will come upon you, and the power of the
Highest will overshadow you; therefore, also, that
Holy One who is to be born will be called the Son of
God" (Luke 1:35).

That's how!

According to the angel, this unique conception was the
work of *the Holy Spirit.*

Another Old Testament prophet named Micah added
this new detail—the predicted Coming One would be
born inside the tiny town of Bethlehem, which lies about

five miles south of Jerusalem. Now don't miss this point—Micah predicted this *nearly 700 years before Jesus was born.* His prophecy declared:

> *But you, **Bethlehem** Ephrathah,*
>
> *Though you are little among the thousands of Judah,*
>
> *Yet out of you shall come forth to Me*
>
> *The One to be Ruler in Israel,*
>
> *Whose goings forth are from of old,*
>
> *From everlasting* (Micah 5:2).

Approximately nine months after Mary's encounter with the angel, the New Testament reports that *"Jesus was born in Bethlehem of Judea in the days of Herod the king"* (Matt. 2:1). Bingo. Micah said it. Jesus fulfilled it. Honestly, can you think of any other human being who can legitimately claim that his birthplace was pinpointed *700 years* in advance?

There is no one but Jesus.

Bethlehem is a big tourist attraction today—for good reason.

Isaiah also predicted the Promised One would live in the vicinity of *"Galilee of the Gentiles"* and would bring *"great light"* to those who *"dwelt in the land of the shadow of death"* (Isa. 9:1-2). The New Testament later reports that Jesus did in fact grow up in *"the region of Galilee...in a city called Nazareth"* (Matt. 2:22-23).

> ***That it might be fulfilled*** *which was spoken by Isaiah the prophet, saying:*
>
> *"The land of Zebulun and the land of Naphtali,*
>
> *By the way of the sea, beyond the Jordan,*
>
> *Galilee of the Gentiles:*
>
> *The people who sat in darkness have seen a great light,*
>
> *And upon those who sat in the region and shadow of death*
>
> *Light has dawned"* (Matthew 4:14-16).

Nearly 600 years before Christ's time, Daniel predicted this long-awaited "Messiah the Prince" would appear publicly near the close of a 70-week, 490-day-for-a-year time prophecy (see Dan. 9:24-27). In the New Testament, in the year A.D. 27, shortly after His public baptism in the river Jordan, Jesus announced:

> ***The time is fulfilled****, and the kingdom of God is at hand. Repent, and believe in the gospel* (Mark 1:15).

In the 400s B.C., Zechariah predicted that Israel's future King would humbly ride into Jerusalem on a lowly donkey (see Zech. 9:9). Jesus did exactly that (see Matt. 21). The New Testament reports:

*All this was done **that it might be fulfilled** which was spoken by the prophet, saying:*

"Tell the daughter of Zion,

'Behold, your King is coming to you,

Lowly, and sitting on a donkey,

A colt, the foal of a donkey'" (Matthew 21:4-5).

Zechariah also predicted that the future Messiah would be betrayed for *"thirty pieces of silver"* (Zech. 11:12-13). One of Christ's own disciples, named Judas, did exactly that. The New Testament reports:

*Then Judas, His betrayer, seeing that He had been condemned, was remorseful and brought back **the thirty pieces of silver** to the chief priests and elders... saying, "I have sinned by betraying innocent blood." ... Then was **fulfilled what was spoken**..."And they took the thirty pieces of silver, the value of Him who was priced, whom they of the children of Israel priced"* (Matthew 27:3,4,9).

Near the end of His earthly life, during His public trial, the Roman governor Pontius Pilate openly confessed, *"I find no fault in Him"* (John 19:4). The reason Pilate found no fault in Jesus was because there was no fault in Jesus. During an earlier encounter with His enemies, Christ innocently inquired, *"Which of you convicts Me of sin?"* (John 8:46). His life was 100 percent flawless. He never cursed, got drunk, acted improperly, lied, or even spoke a false word. Not once. Honestly, no other human being can legitimately claim such spotless sinlessness.

Not one.

Jesus Christ's flawless morality was also predicted by Isaiah the prophet who, after describing His unjust treatment, added:

> *He had done no violence,*
>
> *Nor was any deceit in His mouth* (Isaiah 53:9).

Approximately 1000 B.C., King David predicted that the future Sufferer would be enclosed by a band of wicked men, that His hands and feet would be unjustly pierced, and that certain individuals would cast lots for His clothes (see Ps. 22:16-18). The New Testament reports that after Jesus was rejected by the Jewish Sanhedrin, given over to death by Pontius Pilate, and then handed over to rude Roman soldiers:

*Then they crucified Him, and divided His garments, casting lots, **that it might be fulfilled** which was spoken by the prophet:*

"They divided My garments among them,

And for My clothing they cast lots" (Matthew 27:35).

In the book of Isaiah, chapter 53, many details are given about how a humble, suffering Servant would be despised, rejected, taken prisoner, unjustly *"cut off from the land of the living,"* be buried in the tomb of a rich man, and yet after that, *"He shall prolong His days"* and see again (Isa. 53:3,6,8-11)! In other words, He would *rise from the dead*. Verifiable history reveals that each of these minute prophetic details were literally fulfilled by Jesus (see Matt. 26:23; 27:57; 28:1-8). After His resurrection, the Risen One told His wondering disciples:

*"These are the words which I spoke to you while I was still with you, that **all things must be fulfilled** which were written in the Law of Moses and the Prophets and the Psalms **concerning Me**." And He opened their understanding, that they might comprehend the Scriptures. Then He said to them, "Thus it is written, and thus **it was necessary for the Christ to suffer and to rise from the dead the third day**, and that repentance and remission of*

*sins should be preached in His name to all nations, beginning at Jerusalem. **And you are witnesses of these things**" (Luke 24:44-48).*

Is this really true?

Did Jesus Christ—who I am calling "The Prophecy Man"—*really* rise from the dead?

Consider this—four different historical accounts (Matthew, Mark, Luke, and John) all testify that Jesus lived, taught, and was publicly crucified by Roman soldiers. After six hours of awful suffering on a splintery cross, soldiers *"came to Jesus and saw that He was already dead"* (John 19:33). His body was then taken off the cross, prepared for burial, and placed in a cold, clammy cave just outside the gates of Jerusalem (see Matt. 27:57-61).

After Jesus' body was placed in the cave, *"a large stone"* was rolled over its entrance (Matt. 27:60). Because His enemies wanted to make sure His disciples didn't remove that stone, steal His dead body, and then falsely claim He was resurrected, they persuaded Pontius Pilate to post a guard of Roman soldiers outside the cave (see Matt. 27:62-66). At that point, Jesus' remaining disciples were utterly downcast. Their Master was dead. They went into hiding. But a short time later, something of such historical magnitude happened that it suddenly transformed that utterly devastated band of dejected Jews into fearless men and women willing to die for their faith.

Think about it. If Jesus' disciples had snatched His dead body out of that cave, why would they fearlessly be willing *to die for a lie?* (Most of them were later executed for their faith.) And how could they have gotten past those burly Roman guards, who might be executed if they failed at their specific assignment of protecting Christ's dead body.

It's not logical.

Nevertheless, the tomb was empty!

Not only that, but in the following weeks, over 500 eyewitnesses *saw* the Risen One (see 1 Cor. 15:6). The Bible says that Jesus *"shewed himself alive after his passion* [suffering] *by many infallible proofs"* (Acts 1:3 KJV). Forty days after His resurrection, the Bible then records that in full view of His wondering disciples:

While they [His disciples] *watched, He was taken up, and a cloud received Him out of their sight. And while they looked steadfastly toward heaven as He went up, behold, two men stood by them in white apparel, who also said, "Men of Galilee, why do you stand gazing up into heaven? This same Jesus, who was taken up from you into heaven, will so come in like manner as you saw Him go into heaven"* (Acts 1:9-11).

More on that last part later.

After His ascension, the historical Jesus simply vanished from the pages of history. He was gone. No body. No remains. Nothing. But that was far from the end of His story. History records that Christianity became unstoppable and spread like wildfire throughout the Roman Empire, in spite of incredible opposition and bloody persecution from Roman emperors like Nero (A.D. 37–68), Decius (A.D. 201–251), and Diocletian (A.D. 244–311).

Today, Christianity is *the largest religion in the world.*

Inquiring minds have soberly pondered these historical realities for nearly two thousand years, and skeptics have done their best to disprove them. But they've failed. The evidence still stands. Honestly, the only logical explanation for these astonishing facts is that Jesus Christ *really did rise from the dead.* After looking objectively at these verifiable historical circumstances, bestselling author Josh McDowell, in his book *The Resurrection Factor,* concludes that the case for Christ's resurrection would pass the rigors of any objective court of law.

Nearly two thousand years later, His teachings still have power to transform human hearts. Countless people today can testify that the words of Jesus Christ recorded in the New Testament books of Matthew, Mark, Luke, and John have delivered them from addictive habits, discouragement, fear, despair, and hopelessness into a new life filled with meaning, renewed purpose, hope for the future, and the wondrous assurance that there truly is a God in heaven who created our universe and who loves them deeply—in spite of their sins and faults.

Here is another famous reading summarizing the incredible impact of history's Monumental Man:

> A child is born in an obscure village. He is brought up in another obscure village. He works in a carpenter shop until he is thirty, and then for three brief years is an itinerant preacher, proclaiming a message and living a life. He never writes a book. He never holds an office. He never raises an army. He never has a family of his own. He never owns a home. He never goes to college. He never travels two hundred miles from the place where he was born. He gathers a little group of friends about him and teaches them his way of life. While still a young man, the tide of popular feeling turns against him. One denies him; another betrays him. He is turned over to his enemies. He goes through the mockery of a trial; he is nailed to a cross between two thieves, and when

dead is laid in a borrowed grave by the kindness of a friend.

Those are the facts of his human life. He rises from the dead. Today we look back across nineteen hundred years and ask, What kind of trail has he left across the centuries? When we try to sum up his influence, all the armies that ever marched, all the parliaments that ever sat, all the kings that ever reigned are absolutely picayune in their influence on mankind compared with that of this one solitary life.[1]

In light of the fact that the Holy Bible remains the world's bestselling book, that Jesus Christ is history's most famous Person, and that Christianity itself is the world's largest religion, doesn't it make sober sense to at least consider what Jesus and other biblical prophecies have to say about the times in which we live?

I think so!

NOTE

1. James Allan Francis, "Arise Sir Knight!" in *The Real Jesus and Other Sermons* (Philadelphia, PA: Judson Press, 1926), 123-124.

CHAPTER 2

AN ANCIENT KING'S DREAM

> "I am God, and there is none like Me, declaring the
> end from the beginning, and from ancient times
> things that are not yet done."
>
> —Isaiah 46:9-10

The Holy Bible claims to be an inspired book that was written not through the ingenuity or craftiness of men, but by *"holy men of God* [who] *spoke as they were moved by the Holy Spirit"* (2 Pet. 1:21). In this chapter, I will zero in on one ancient biblical prophecy that has been strikingly fulfilled in the pages of real human history.

The year was approximately 605 B.C. Daniel was a Jewish captive snatched from Jerusalem during the reign of one of ancient Babylon's greatest rulers—King

Nebuchadnezzar (634–562 B.C.). Because Daniel was intelligent, of royal lineage, and showed great promise to the Babylonian administration, he and three of his close friends were carefully selected to be part of a wise-men-in-training group being groomed to serve the king (see Dan. 1). Interestingly enough, most of Nebuchadnezzar's regular advisors were sorcerers.

One dark night, *"in the second year of Nebuchadnezzar's reign, Nebuchadnezzar had dreams; and his spirit was so troubled that his sleep left him"* (Dan. 2:1). Waking up in a cold sweat and sensing he had dreamed something deeply important, the king became frustrated as its foggy memory slipped beyond his awareness into realms unknown.

I must get that dream back! he told himself. *But how? Who can help me? Ah, my trusted wise men!*

Then the king gave the command to call the magicians, the astrologers, the sorcerers, and the Chaldeans to tell the king his dreams. So they came and stood before the king. And the king said to them, "I have had a dream, and my spirit is anxious to know the dream." Then the Chaldeans spoke to the king in Aramaic, "O king, live forever! Tell your servants the dream, and we will give the interpretation." The king answered and said to the Chaldeans, "My decision is firm: if you do not make known the dream to me, and its interpretation, you shall be cut in pieces, and your houses shall be made an ash heap. However, if you tell the dream and its interpretation, you shall receive from me gifts, rewards, and great honor. Therefore tell me the dream and its interpretation" (Daniel 2:2-6).

King Nebuchadnezzar wanted his star-gazing advisors to tell him both the dream and its meaning, thus proving their self-proclaimed ability to access secret knowledge, but they couldn't. The sorcerers were stumped! They answered again and said:

"Let the king tell his servants the dream, and we will give its interpretation." The king answered and said, "I know for certain that you would gain time, because you see that my decision is firm: if you do not make known the dream to me, there is only one decree for you! For you have agreed to speak lying and corrupt words before me till the time has changed. Therefore tell me the dream, and I shall know that you can give me its interpretation" (Daniel 2:7-9).

This was no fictitious encounter. King Nebuchadnezzar had a fiery temper, especially if he sensed he had been hoodwinked by shysters. Now the lives of these magicians were at stake. It was do or die, put up or shut up—and have their heads cut off. They couldn't perform. Their claim to hidden insights proved false. With knocking knees, they responded again to the hot-under-the-collar king:

> *There is not a man on earth who can tell the king's matter; therefore no king, lord, or ruler has ever asked such things of any magician, astrologer, or Chaldean. It is a difficult thing that the king requests, and there is no other who can tell it to the king except the gods, whose dwelling is not with flesh* (Daniel 2:10-11).

In desperation, the magic-makers even blamed their sovereign ruler for making an unreasonable request. Big mistake. Nebuchadnezzar didn't appreciate such remarks.

> *For this reason the king was angry and very furious, and gave a command to destroy all the wise men of Babylon. So the decree went out, and they began killing the wise men; and they sought Daniel and his companions, to kill them* (Daniel 2:12-13).

Executioners soon showed up at Daniel's door too, because he and his friends were counted among the king's wise men. Yet because Daniel had developed a friendship with the captain of the king's guard, he was allowed to seek a solution that might save his life.

Then with counsel and wisdom Daniel answered Arioch, the captain of the king's guard, who had gone out to kill the wise men of Babylon; he answered and said to Arioch the king's captain, "Why is the decree from the king so urgent?" Then Arioch made the decision known to Daniel. So Daniel went in and asked the king to give him time, that he might tell the king the interpretation. Then Daniel went to his house, and made the decision known to Hananiah, Mishael, and Azariah, his companions, that they might seek mercies from the God of heaven concerning this secret, so that Daniel and his companions might not perish with the rest of the wise men of Babylon (Daniel 2:14-18).

The occultists had tried their crystal balls, tarot cards, tea leaves, astrological charts, and divination techniques, but nothing worked. But Daniel had direct access to a superior Source of assistance unknown to magicians. His trust was in the living God *"who made heaven and earth"* (Ps. 121:2). That night Daniel knelt quietly by his bed, said a prayer, and then drifted peacefully to sleep trusting in his heavenly Father. His faith was soon rewarded.

Then the secret was revealed to Daniel in a night vision. So Daniel blessed the God of heaven. Daniel answered and said:

"Blessed be the name of God forever and ever,

For wisdom and might are His.

And He changes the times and the seasons;

He removes kings and raises up kings;

He gives wisdom to the wise

And knowledge to those who have understanding.

He reveals deep and secret things;

He knows what is in the darkness,

And light dwells with Him.

I thank You and praise You,

O God of my fathers;

You have given me wisdom and might,

And have now made known to me what we asked of You,

For You have made known to us the king's demand"
(Daniel 2:19-23).

Daniel knew the answer didn't come from himself, nature, cauldrons, concentration, spirits, or heavenly goddesses—but from God alone. After gratefully thanking the Eternal Revealer, he hastened back to the nervous sergeant.

Therefore Daniel went to Arioch, whom the king had appointed to destroy the wise men of Babylon. He went and said thus to him: "Do not destroy the wise men of Babylon; take me before the king, and I will tell the king the interpretation" (Daniel 2:24).

"Take me before the king" indeed! Arioch happily complied. To the palace Daniel went, past meticulously manicured and blossoming gardens, bubbling waterfalls, glistening corridors, and into the throne room of the greatest monarch on earth at the time. Try to picture the scene—a lone Jew stood before a mighty Babylonian ruler. The Bible reports:

Then Arioch quickly brought Daniel before the king, and said thus to him, "I have found a man of the captives of Judah, who will make known to the king the interpretation." The king answered and said to Daniel, whose [Babylonian] name was Belteshazzar, "Are you able to make known to me the dream which I have seen, and its interpretation?" (Daniel 2:25-26)

The crucial moment had come. Well? Could Daniel discern both the dream *and* its meaning, or was his knowledge of hidden realities no better than sorcerers? Nebuchadnezzar and Arioch waited breathlessly.

Daniel answered in the presence of the king, and said, "The secret which the king has demanded, the wise men, the astrologers, the magicians, and the soothsayers cannot declare to the king. But there is a God in heaven who reveals secrets, and He has made known to King Nebuchadnezzar what will be in the latter days" (Daniel 2:27-28).

This passage is filled with true wisdom. Daniel reminded Nebuchadnezzar that all of his Babylonian wise men, magicians, astrologers, and occult practitioners were clueless about the dream and its interpretation. They were as useless as paying $100,000 to a palm reader. Then Daniel divulged the golden key: *"There is a God in heaven who reveals secrets."* Ah yes, the Almighty has answers! The Lord gave the dream, and then He explained its mysteries to His humble servant. Daniel took no credit for the insight; it wasn't because he had mastered any complex techniques or practices. He simply prayed, and God answered. Again, Daniel stressed that the answer didn't come because he was smart or special but because he trusted God's mercy:

But as for me, this secret has not been revealed to me because I have more wisdom than anyone living, but for our sakes who make known the interpretation to the king, and that you may know the thoughts of your heart (Daniel 2:30).

"More wisdom" is what contemporary occultists claim, too. In fact, the word *occult* means "hidden knowledge." Occult practitioners think they understand hidden knowledge, while those who don't are ignorant "muggles"—to borrow a term from the *Harry Potter* novels. Yet Daniel 2 reveals that the supposed wisdom of sorcerers is foolishness. Real knowledge comes from the true Creator of heaven and earth. *"The fear of the Lord is the beginning of knowledge, but fools despise wisdom and instruction"* (Prov. 1:7).

As King Nebuchadnezzar sat on the edge of his glistening throne, Daniel respectfully told him what he dreamed:

You, O king, were watching; and behold, a great image! This great image, whose splendor was excellent, stood before you; and its form was awesome. This image's head was of fine gold, its chest and arms of silver, its belly and thighs of bronze, its legs of iron, its feet partly of iron and partly of clay. You watched while a stone was cut out without hands, which struck the image on its feet of iron and clay, and broke them in pieces. Then the iron, the clay, the bronze, the silver, and the gold were crushed together, and became like chaff from the summer threshing floors; the wind carried them away so that no trace of them was found. And the stone that struck the

image became a great mountain and filled the whole
earth. This is the dream (Daniel 2:31-36).

"That's it!" Nebuchadnezzar probably blurted out, nearly falling off his throne. Leaning forward earnestly, he may have asked anxiously, "But what does it mean?" Now follow closely. Daniel's reply concerns the entire human race—including the proponents of today's numerous religions, all sorcerers, plus you and me too. His message reaches down to the end of time:

Now we will tell the interpretation of it before the king.
You, O king, are a king of kings. For the God of heaven
has given you a kingdom, power, strength, and glory;
and wherever the children of men dwell, or the beasts
of the field and the birds of the heaven, He has given
them into your hand, and has made you ruler over
them all—you are this head of gold (Daniel 2:36-38).

Daniel stated that the golden head on the metallic image Nebuchadnezzar saw in his foggy dream represented both the king and his Babylonian kingdom. *"You are this head of gold."*

Historically, Babylon was known for its gold. Nicknamed "the golden city," the poet Aeschylus (525–456 B.C.) said it was "teeming with gold." The famous Greek historian Herodotus (484-425 B.C.) visited Babylon around 90 years after Nebuchadnezzar's era and wondered at the amount of gold inside the city. Babylon's walls and buildings glistened with gold. Entering the Ishtar Gate and walking down Procession Street would take a visitor to the Temple of Marduk (Babylon's primary god) that supported a 40-foot golden statue of Marduk rising near a golden chair, golden table, and golden altar. Thus, Daniel's words to Nebuchadnezzar, "You are this head of gold," fit perfectly with real history.

King Nebuchadnezzar himself was Babylon's primary builder (see Dan. 4:30). He hoped his golden empire would last forever, but it was not to be. The humble Jewish prophet continued:

> *But after you shall arise another kingdom inferior to yours; then another, a third kingdom of bronze, which shall rule over all the earth* (Daniel 2:39).

Here Daniel revealed "the secret" that Nebuchadnezzar's dream was actually a prophecy of the rise and fall of nations. *"After you shall arise another kingdom inferior to yours."* So it was. In 538 B.C., Babylonia fell to Persia—a nation represented by the breast and silver arms of the image in Nebuchadnezzar's dream. Historically, Persia was known for its silver. It used silver coins for commerce.

"Then another, a third kingdom of bronze...shall rule over all the earth." In 331 B.C., Alexander the Great mercilessly crushed Persia's army in the name of Greece at the battle of Arbela, even though his troops were outnumbered twenty to one. But providence was on his side. *The prophecy must be fulfilled.* The ancient Greeks were known for their bronze, fighting their battles with bronze helmets, swords, and shields.

> *And the fourth kingdom shall be as strong as iron, inasmuch as iron breaks in pieces and shatters everything; and like iron that crushes, that kingdom will break in pieces and crush all the others* (Daniel 2:40).

History confirms perfectly that the fourth kingdom after Babylon, Persia, and Greece was Rome, the mightiest nation of them all. The famed historian Edward Gibbon (1737–1794), in his classic volume *History of the Decline and Fall of the Roman Empire,* even used the exact language of biblical prophecy when he wrote about "the iron monarchy of Rome":

> The arms of the [Roman] Republic, sometimes vanquished in battle, always victorious in war, advanced with rapid steps to the Euphrates, the Danube, the Rhine, and

> the ocean; and the images of gold, or silver, or brass, that might serve to represent the nations and their kings, were successively broken by the iron monarchy of Rome.[1]

Roman caesars ruled the civilized world from 168 B.C. to A.D. 476, until the imperial government finally crumbled under vicious assaults of barbarian invaders from the wild territories of northern Germany. From A.D. 476 onward—even to this day—Europe has remained divided, exactly as Nebuchadnezzar's dream predicted. Daniel then told the trembling king:

> *Whereas you saw the feet and toes, partly of potter's clay and partly of iron, the kingdom shall be divided; yet the strength of the iron shall be in it, just as you saw the iron mixed with ceramic clay* (Daniel 2:41).

True to the prophecy, between A.D. 351 and A.D. 476, Rome's kingdom was "divided" into ten smaller nations— Alamani, Burgundians, Anglo-Saxons, Suevi, Visagoths, Lombards, Franks, Vandals, Heruli, and Ostrogoths— most of which eventually became the nations of Europe we see today. That solitary prophetic word, *divided*, accurately describes the state of Europe from the fifth century until now.

And as the toes of the feet were partly of iron and partly of clay, so the kingdom shall be partly strong and partly fragile (Daniel 2:42).

How accurate this prophecy is! Even today, some European nations are strong; some are weak. Some are ironlike; some are softer like clay. It's been this way for 1,500 years. Sometimes "the toes" get along; sometimes they don't. Daniel revealed more precise details:

As you saw iron mixed with ceramic clay, they will mingle with the seed of men (Daniel 2:43).

"Mingle with the seed of men" is a prediction of inter-marriage among the toes—that is, between various royal houses throughout Europe. The purpose of such min-gling was to create alliances so that one toe could finally become the big toe—with the goal in mind of a fully reunited Europe under one government. Simply review European history with its royal weddings, incest, in-laws, and out-laws. It's all predicted in God's Word. Yet for 1,500 years, complete unity has eluded the contestants, for it is written:

But they will not adhere to one another, just as iron does not mix with clay (Daniel 2:43).

As it has been; even so it is now. Throughout European history various kings, monarchs, generals, and dictators have tried to unite Europe under their rule, but they all failed. Charlemagne tried it. Charles V tried it. Louis XIV tried it. So did Kaiser Wilhelm, Napoleon Bonaparte, and Adolf Hitler. Yet Europe remains splintered because God's prophecy predicts, *"they will not adhere to one another, just as iron does not mix with clay."*

Napoleon knew about the prophecy in Daniel 2. When the Little Corporal was finally defeated at the Battle of Waterloo (in 1815), he purportedly said, "God Almighty is too much for me!" During the rise of the Third Reich, Adolf Hitler became ill. While lying upon his sickbed, his attending nurse showed him Nebuchadnezzar's dream and Daniel's interpretation. "This doesn't fit into my plans!" the dictator shouted, throwing the Bible against the wall. But Hitler's cruelty didn't fit into God's plans, and a bullet from his own pistol finally ended his cruel, miserable life.

King Nebuchadnezzar couldn't possibly have foreseen all this, but the One who revealed His secret to Daniel surely did. In the hearing of the awestruck king, the Jewish prophet swiftly approached his climax:

And in the days of these kings the God of heaven will set up a kingdom which shall never be destroyed; and the kingdom shall not be left to other people; it shall break in pieces and consume all these kingdoms, and it shall stand forever (Daniel 2:44).

After the rise and fall of Babylonia, Persia, Greece, and Rome, after centuries of European intermarriage and division, and after all efforts for complete unity have miserably failed, *"the God of heaven will set up a kingdom which shall never be destroyed."* This Kingdom won't have a beginning and ending date to be recorded in some history book. Neither will it take its place among human governments in some sort of cooperative, treaty-based relationship. No. *"It shall break in pieces and consume all these kingdoms, and it shall stand forever."*

The towering metal man in Nebuchadnezzar's cryptic dream represents the kingdoms of men. At the end of this dream, the golden head, silver arms, bronze belly, iron legs, and divided toes are consumed and obliterated entirely. God's kingdom alone will remain. *"It shall stand forever."* Looking the Babylonian monarch squarely in the eyes (which were probably quite wide by now), the Jewish prophet concluded:

Inasmuch as you saw that the stone was cut out of the mountain without hands, and that it broke in pieces the iron, the bronze, the clay, the silver, and the gold—the great God has made known to the king what will come to pass after this. The dream is certain, and its interpretation is sure (Daniel 2:45).

The multi-colored statue is crushed by "the stone" representing God's Kingdom. That boulder is quarried from a mountain "without hands," meaning no human influence is involved. It is wholly divine—a Rock of Ages. The prophecy comes from *"the great God who has made known to the king what will come to pass after this."* No speculation is involved. This prediction doesn't come from some scary ghost speaking through an unconscious medium in a trance. No, it comes from God Himself, as explained by one of His true prophets.

"The dream is certain," Daniel declared, *"and its interpretation is sure."* So far—just like Jesus Christ fulfilled prior biblical prophecies—the rise and fall of nations has also verified the accuracy of this prophecy in real history.

Then King Nebuchadnezzar fell on his face, prostrate before Daniel, and commanded that they should present an offering and incense to him. The king answered Daniel, and said, "Truly your God is the God of gods, the Lord of kings, and a revealer of secrets, since you could reveal this secret." Then the king promoted Daniel and gave him many great gifts; and he made him ruler over the whole province of Babylon, and chief administrator over all the wise men of Babylon (Daniel 2:46-48).

Nebuchadnezzar recognized truth when he heard it. The dream and its interpretation—coming through a humble Jewish prophet—ultimately came from God Almighty, who is far above all magicians, astrologers, sorcerers, mediums, or palm readers. At the very end of human history, when that unstoppable Rock finally strikes the earth, *"it shall break in pieces and consume all these kingdoms, and it shall stand forever"* (Dan. 2:44).

The final shattering will occur on *"the battle of that great day of God Almighty"* (Rev. 16:14). The Book of Revelation—the last book of the Bible—calls this battle, *"Armageddon"* (Rev. 16:16).

Are we *Approaching Armageddon* now?

You will soon find out.

NOTE

1.   Edward Gibbon, J.B. Bury, ed., *The Decline and Fall of the Roman Empire, vol. IV*, qtd. in Peter Gay, ed., *The Enlightenment: A Comprehensive Anthology* (New York,

NY: Touchstone, 1973), 651-660, accessed August 3, 2020, http://www.historyguide.org/intellect/gibbon_decline.html.

CHAPTER 3

"NOT ONE STONE SHALL BE LEFT"

> "That men do not learn very much from the lessons of history is the most important of all the lessons that history has to teach."
>
> —Aldous Huxley, "A Case of Voluntary Ignorance"

A few days before His shameful betrayal by Judas, public trial before Pontius Pilate, and brutal crucifixion by Roman soldiers, Jesus was teaching the people inside a building that had become the Jewish nation's pride and joy—its magnificent temple. Originally built as a movable "tabernacle" by the Israelites during their wilderness wanderings (approximately 1400 B.C.), permanently constructed into one of the wonders of the ancient world by King Solomon (900s B.C.), later rebuilt under the leadership of Zerubbabel (500s B.C.), and finally embellished by Herod the Great (73–4 B.C.), the Jewish temple was the undisputed center of first-century Judaism.

"Then Jesus went out and departed from the temple, and His disciples came up to show Him the buildings of the temple" (Matt. 24:1). "Isn't our temple beautiful?" Christ's disciples may have asked. "Look at those massive walls of white marble!" Yet a sense of foreboding filled their minds. A short time earlier, Jesus had told the Pharisees, *"See! Your house is left to you desolate"* (Matt. 23:38).

Desolate?

What did the Master mean by that?

Jesus read their unspoken thoughts (which He did regularly) and spoke words that must have shocked them:

Do you not see all these things? Assuredly, I say to you, not one stone shall be left here upon another, that shall not be thrown down (Matthew 24:2).

Those Jewish men could hardly believe their ears. "Not one stone shall be left" of God's temple? *Is this possible?* Their heads must have been spinning. Absorbed in troubled thought, they silently followed their Master as He meandered through Jerusalem's dusty streets, through an eastern gate, over a creek, and up the western slope of the Mount of Olives.

Jesus then seated Himself on a comfortable spot overlooking the city. His disciples could hardly contain themselves any longer. They just had to ask the Teacher for more inside information about their beloved temple. Did His prediction concern the Last Day? The Bible continues:

> Now as He sat on the Mount of Olives, the disciples came to Him privately, saying, "Tell us, when will these things be? And what will be the sign of Your coming, and of the end of the age?" (Matthew 24:3)

The first part of their question, *"Tell us, when will these things be?"* concerned Christ's unexpected prediction about the destruction of the temple. *If our temple is doomed,* they must have thought, *surely this would occur at history's Great Climax.* This led to the second part of their question, *"And what will be the sign of Your coming, and of the end of the age?"* Notice carefully. The disciples asked Jesus for clarification about three things:

1 The destruction of the Jewish Temple

2. The sign of His Second Coming

3. The end of the age

In this chapter, I'm going to focus on point 1. Later chapters will highlight point 2—*signs* of the approaching Grand Finale, leading to *the* sign of His return. Near the end of this book, I will zero in on point 3—the meaning of "the end of the age," which the King James Version of the Bible translates as "the end of the world."

As we've already seen in Chapter 1, Jesus Himself fulfilled multiple Old Testament prophecies pointing forward to minute details about His birth, birthplace, hometown, life, betrayal, sufferings, crucifixion, death, and resurrection. We've also seen in Chapter 2 that Daniel the prophet accurately explained King Nebuchadnezzar's dream foreshadowing the rise and fall of four mighty nations—Babylonia, Persia, Greece, and Rome—predictions that have been accurately and verifiably fulfilled on the pages of actual history. In this chapter we shall see another definite fulfillment of Bible prophecy that will give us further confidence in the accuracy of God's Book.

It was in the spring of A.D. 31 when Jesus first declared, "not one stone shall be left" of the Jewish temple. At that moment, Jerusalem itself—built high on a hill—was still surrounded by steep walls and strong towers. It seemed impregnable. It's golden-laced temple also still glistened in the sun. There was no sign of impending doom. How could there be? The Jews were God's people, right? And hadn't God made rich promises to them in His Word? And wasn't Mount Zion "the Mountain of the Lord of hosts, The Holy Mountain"? (see Zech. 8:3). The answer to all three of these questions is yes.

Yet other factors must be considered. In the prophecy of Daniel 9:24-27 referred to earlier, the angel Gabriel predicted that *"Messiah"* would be *"cut off"* (Dan. 9:26). In other words, Jesus would be rejected by the majority of the Jewish leaders and eventually crucified. These events would bring such guilt upon the Jewish nation and her rulers that God would finally allow fierce Roman legions to not only attack, but to *"destroy the city* [Jerusalem] *and the sanctuary* [Israel's temple]" (Dan. 9:26). Gabriel also added that this catastrophe would result in utter "desolations." It was this exact prophecy in Daniel 9:26 that Jesus referred to when He told the Pharisees, *"See! Your house is left to you desolate"* (Matt. 23:38). In a parallel prophecy, Jesus also told His disciples:

> *When you see Jerusalem surrounded by armies, then know that its desolation is near. Then let those who are in Judea flee to the mountains, let those who are in the midst of her depart, and let not those who are in the country enter her. For these are the days of*

*vengeance, that all things which are written **may be fulfilled*** (Luke 21:20-22).

Again, remember, Jesus first gave this prediction in the spring of A.D. 31 at a time when there was absolutely *no evidence* at that moment that such a prophecy could *ever be fulfilled.* Imagine someone predicting today, "Forty years from now, America will vanish. I'm going to give you a sign. Watch for it. When you see that sign in forty years, catch the next flight to Europe!"

The predictor would be labeled a lunatic!

Yet it was Jesus Christ Himself who made this prediction. It came from lips that never lie. Prophecy, and fulfillment, was His special forte. As I briefly describe what happened, you can Google each point. Do your homework. Check the dates. The history is easily verifiable for all the world to see. The facts prove that, once again, Jesus Christ told the truth.

Again, *He never lies.*

In Luke 21:20-22 quoted above, Jesus made these four predictions:

1. Jerusalem was to be "surrounded by armies."
2. This would indicate that "its desolation" was near.

3. Before the onslaught, there would be a providential opportunity for Christ's followers to "flee to the mountains" so they could avoid the pending ruin.

4. The coming destruction would occur "that all things which are written [in the prophecy of Daniel 9:26] *may be fulfilled.*"

There is no doubt that Jesus Christ's pointed predictions were perfectly and literally fulfilled nearly 40 years after He spoke them. Again, just think about it. If someone made such a prediction today—which included specific details—how likely is it that those details would be exactly fulfilled 40 years later? But this was precisely the case with the words of Jesus Christ.[1]

One reason why the Jewish Sanhedrin (Israel's ruling body in the first century) rejected Jesus was because He didn't fit their view of what their promised Messiah was supposed to do. "Our Messiah will annihilate the hated Romans," they told the common people, "and set us free." But Jesus didn't come to do that. Instead, His mission was to humbly sacrifice Himself to pay the price for human sin, to forgive sinners, to change their hearts, to teach about the transforming power of the Holy Spirit, and to instill within His followers a new love for everyone—including Romans.

The Jewish rulers weren't interested in that.

They were expecting a lion, a warrior king like David, not a Messiah who came like a lowly lamb (see Isa. 53:7; John 1:29).

So most rejected Jesus and His free gift of salvation.

After Christ's public, unjust trials before the Sanhedrin, King Herod, and Pontius Pilate—and after His bloody crucifixion, death, glorious resurrection, and visible ascension to heaven—Christianity spread like wildfire throughout the Roman Empire. Significantly, the earliest Christians were mostly Jews who believed in Jesus (see Acts 2:5,9-11,14,41-47). Tragically, many of their initial persecutors were other Jews who stubbornly refused to accept that Jesus was their Messiah (see Acts 4:1-21; 5:17-42; 6:9-8:4; 9:1,2; 12:1-4; 14:19; 17:5; 20:3; 21:26-32; 23:12-24).

After *"He* [Jesus] *was received up into heaven, and sat down at the right hand of God"* (Mark 16:19), and at the same time that Christianity was rapidly spreading throughout Judea, Asia Minor, and even Europe, tensions kept mounting between the Romans and the unbelieving Jews, whose headquarters was in Jerusalem. Remember, unbelieving Jews were still hoping for a military Messiah who would overthrow their national enemies. In the years following Christ's ascension, this expectation grew.

A radical, militant Jewish faction, known as "the Zealots," often attacked and killed Roman soldiers. Reprisals against Jews were swift and often bloody. By A.D. 66, Rome's patience had expired. It was time for war.

The First Jewish-Roman War started in A.D. 66 and ended in A.D. 73 and resulted in massive destruction among the Jewish people. Even the Temple was destroyed—the symbol and center of all Jewish life.

In A.D. 66, in the twelfth year of Nero, the Roman general Cestius Gallus attacked Jerusalem. Just as Jesus predicted 35 years earlier, "Jerusalem [was] surrounded by armies."

> The Roman army [under Cestius Gallus] reached Scopus, seized the suburbs of Jerusalem, and besieged the Temple Mount. A few days later, however, Cestius decided to withdraw. ...Cestius' decision may have resulted from a pessimistic appraisal of his army's strength or of the logistics situation in the light of the approaching winter.[2]

The exact reason for Cestius' choice remains shrouded in mystery. No one really knows for sure why he pulled back from Jerusalem. But we do know that Jesus not only predicted that Jerusalem would be "surrounded by armies," but also that somehow, for some reason, in the midst of the siege a window of opportunity would unexpectedly open for His followers still inside Jerusalem to get out safely.

This is exactly what happened. When Cestius unexpectedly withdrew his army, Jewish zealots inside Jerusalem misinterpreted this as a sign of God's favor.

They were wrong.

Instead, it was a sign of pending desolation.

Jerusalem's bolted gates opened, and Jewish warriors rushed out of the city in hot pursuit. The rebels were able to successfully push the Romans back, and a full-scale war was officially under way. Unfortunately for the Jewish people, it was not a war they were going to win.

Now here's the critical part—when Cestius unexpectedly withdrew and Jerusalem's gates opened, and when the zealots hurriedly pursued the Romans, the waiting Christians recognized the promised sign. *This is it!* they whispered earnestly to each other. *Time to get out—now!*

Jesus had told them:

Then *let those who are in Judea flee to the mountains* (Luke 21:21).

Obedient to their Lord's command, the Christians acted fast. In the confusion, most Jews hardly noticed.

Without even packing their belongings, every Christian inside Jerusalem quickly escaped through the open gates, fleeing to the small town of Pella, nestled within the eastern foothills of the Jordan Valley. Miraculously, no Christians perished in the subsequent bloodbath.

The lesson for us is clear.

We should listen carefully to what Jesus says!

In this instance, the zealots were victorious. No one knows the exact count, but estimates are that between 5,000 and 6,000 Roman soldiers were slaughtered. Victoriously returning to Jerusalem (after the Jewish Christians left), the city gates were once again closed shut. Yet this unexpected defeat only further enraged the Romans against the Jews.

Three and a half years later, in A.D. 70, the Romans returned. The date was April 14. Unfortunately, this was at the beginning of the Passover season when Jerusalem was packed with nearly a million pilgrims. This time, the siege was resumed by the Roman general Titus (A.D. 39–81) who, nine years later, became emperor of Rome. At the start of this siege, Titus quickly cut off all escape. This time, there would be no Jewish victory. As Jesus predicted, the utter desolation of Israel's sacred city and magnificent temple was truly near (see Luke 21:20).

The details are tragic and gory. The historian Josephus, himself an eyewitness of the tragedy, spares few details. The siege lasted for about four months. When food supplies started running out within the city, the horror intensified. Countless Jews who tried to escape were captured and crucified beneath the city walls. The number of crosses was so great there was scarcely room to move among them. Within the city, fighting, rage, and murder were common. Some even resorted to cannibalism. When the Romans finally broke through those immense walls, the carnage was unimaginable.

> As the [Roman] legions charged in, neither persuasion nor threat could check their impetuosity: passion alone was in command. Crowded together around the entrances many were trampled by their friends, many fell among the still hot and smoking ruins of the colonnades and died as miserably as the defeated. As they neared the Sanctuary they pretended not even to hear Caesar's commands and urged the men in front to throw in more firebrands. The partisans were no longer in a position to help; everywhere was slaughter and flight. Most of the victims were peaceful citizens,

weak and unarmed, butchered wherever they were caught. Round the Altar the heaps of corpses grew higher and higher, while down the Sanctuary steps poured a river of blood and the bodies of those killed at the top slithered to the bottom.[3]

As Roman troops edged closer to the Temple itself, Titus desired to save the magnificent structure from utter ruin. According to Josephus, it was the Jews who first used fire in the Northwest approach to the Temple to try to stop the Roman advances. Only then did Roman soldiers set fire to an apartment adjacent to the Temple, starting a conflagration which the Jews subsequently made worse.

Realizing that there was still time to save the glorious edifice, Titus dashed out and by personal efforts strove to persuade his men to put out the fire...but their respect for Caesar and their fear of the centurion's staff were powerless against their fury. ... Thus the Sanctuary was set on fire in defiance of Caesar's wishes.[4]

As the Roman legions entered the temple precincts, they mercilessly slaughtered men, women, and children who had taken refuge within. As they looked around, the soldiers saw what looked like gold everywhere, which only further fueled their madness to find treasures within. A Roman soldier tossed in a lighted torch. Within seconds, the entire structure burst into unquenchable flames. In the intense heat, stores of gold and silver, which had been placed inside the temple for safe keeping, literally melted and ran down between the stones. Roman soldiers tore apart those stones to retrieve the gold, literally leaving "not one stone left."

Small companies on surrounding hillsides watched with breathless silence as the entire summit blazed like a volcano. When the fires finally went out and the dust settled, both the temple and the city were completely destroyed and left desolate, exactly as the angel Gabriel and as Jesus predicted. Nothing was left. Over a million Jews perished.

Some speculate that the Western Wall, which is still visible inside Jerusalem's Old City, is a remnant of Israel's temple, but there is no real evidence for this. Instead, the consensus is that it is simply a retaining wall to stop falling rocks and dirt below the old temple mount. In his scholarly book *The Archaeology of the Jerusalem Area*, Harold Mare, former president of the Near East Archaeological Society, clarifies:

> *We do not have any remains of the Herodian temple itself* because of the devastating Roman destruction in A.D. 70.[5]

Professor Mare is correct. Herod's temple was completely demolished, *just as Jesus predicted.*

What else do Jesus Christ and the Holy Bible predict about the future? Are there any present-day "signs" that we are truly *Approaching Armageddon?*

It's almost time to find out.

NOTES

1. If you have an interest in doing more research, these astonishing events were recorded in great detail by Flavius Josephus (A.D. 37–100) in his classic work *The War of the Jews.*

2. Lea Roth, "Cestius Gallus," Encyclopedia.com, August 24, 2020, https://www.encyclopedia.com/religion/ encyclopedias-almanacs-transcripts-and-maps/cestius -gallusdeg.

3. Flavius Josephus, G.A. Williamson, trans., *The War of the Jews* (London: Penguin Classics, 1981), 358.

4. Ibid.

5. Harold Mare, *The Archaeology of the Jerusalem Area* (Grand Rapids: Baker, 1987), 141.

CHAPTER 4

"I WILL COME AGAIN"

> "Begin with the end in mind."
>
> —Stephen Covey,
> *7 Habits of Highly Effective People*

Have you heard the saying, "Cleanliness is next to godliness"? Here's another saying: "Simplicity is the path to truth." Personally, I appreciate easy-to-grasp, simple information. In this chapter, I hope to make Bible truth as simple as possible.

When the disciples asked Jesus, *"Tell us, when will these things be?"* (Matt. 24:3), we have already discovered that they wanted to know when "not one stone would be left" of the Jewish temple. In the last chapter, we also learned that Christ's prediction was perfectly fulfilled nearly forty years later, in A.D. 70, when both Jerusalem and its temple were demolished by Roman legions led by Prince Titus.

The disciples also inquired, *"and what will be the sign of Your coming, and of the end of the age?"* Those two words, "Your coming," refer to the return of Jesus Christ. The disciples associated His return with "the end of the age." As we all know, Jesus came the first time nearly two thousand years ago. Will He come again? If so, can we know when His return is near? And what about *"the end of the world"* (KJV)? Will there truly be an "end" to life on earth as we know it? To discover the facts, we should let the Truth Teller answer those questions.

Our Savior's lengthy answer starts in the next verse (in Matthew 24:4) and continues all the way to the end of Matthew 25. After listing numerous signs, trends, and events He knew would come, Jesus said:

> *All these things must come to pass, but **the end** is not yet* (Matthew 24:6).

> *But he who endures to **the end** shall be saved* (Matthew 24:13).

> *And this gospel of the kingdom will be preached in all the world as a witness to all the nations, and then **the end** will come* (Matthew 24:14).

Here Jesus spoke of "the end" *three times* in just a few sentences. First, "the end is not yet." Next, "he who endures to the end." Finally, "and then the end will come." If we take His words at face value, there is no doubt that Jesus believed that "the end" would eventually come.

For the sake of simplicity, we could say that the Bible identifies *three monumental events*:

1. The Creation of planet Earth
2. The First Coming of Jesus Christ
3. The Second Coming of Jesus Christ

Again, for the sake of simplicity, think of it this way: Every basketball or football game has a starting point when the game officially begins. Then there is half-time. Finally, there are the closing moments, and then the game officially ends. When the last buzzer sounds, there are both winners and losers, which is determined by how the players played the game.

It's the same with history. The official starting point began when, *"In the beginning God created the heavens and the earth"* (Gen. 1:1). We might say that "half-time" occurred when Jesus entered our world, successfully fulfilled His holy mission, paid the price for human sin, rose from the dead, and then ascended back to heaven (see

Acts 1:9-11). At this moment, we are still waiting for *the end of the game* when He will return to wrap things up.

When that Day arrives, each of us will either be a winner or a loser, *depending on how we played the game.*

The return of Jesus Christ to this earth isn't a minor doctrine in the Bible. It's major—being much more important than any major a student may choose in college. In fact, for every reference in the Bible to Christ's first coming, there are approximately eight verses about His Second Coming. Not long before His public trial and crucifixion, which He knew would be very difficult for those who loved Him to endure, Jesus told His disciples:

> *Let not your heart be troubled; you believe in God, believe also in Me. In My Father's house are many mansions; if it were not so, I would have told you. I go* [referring to His ascension] *to prepare a place for you. And if I go and prepare a place for you,* **I will come again** [His Second Coming] *and receive you to Myself; that where I am, there you may be also* (John 14:1-3).

That's simple enough. "I will come again," said the Lord. We previously saw the same truth revealed by two holy angels dressed in white garments who suddenly appeared and spoke to the disciples as Jesus ascended back to His Father:

*Now when He had spoken these things, while they watched, He was taken up, and a cloud received Him out of their sight. And while they looked stead-fastly toward heaven as He went up, behold, two men stood by them in white apparel, who also said, "Men of Galilee, why do you stand gazing up into heaven? **This same Jesus, who was taken up from you into heaven, will so come in like manner as you saw Him go into heaven"** (Acts 1:9-11).*

That's simple, too. Jesus was literally "taken up" into heaven in full view of His awestruck disciples. Two holy angels then informed them that "this same Jesus"—meaning the exact same Person who lived, loved, suffered, died, and rose—"will so come in like manner as you saw Him go into heaven." No hazy, mystical, ethereal, non-personal return is being described here.

Instead, Jesus Christ Himself will literally come right down from the sky, just like He went up. If you still have doubts, Jesus' own words in Matthew 24 make this Bible truth exceedingly clear. Remember, the disciples asked Jesus, "and what will be *the sign of Your coming,* and of the end of the age?" Here is His answer:

*Then **the sign** of the Son of Man will appear in heaven, and then all the tribes of the earth will* *mourn, and they will see the Son of Man coming on the clouds of heaven with power and great glory* (Matthew 24:30).

These words are clear as sunlight. "The sign" of Jesus Christ's return will be His literal, visible, apocalyptic, and unimaginably glorious personal appearance in the clouds. No one will wonder, "Is that a bird? Or a plane? Or a satellite? Or a *Star Trek*-type of alien from outer space?" No chance. As His cloud draws closer, "all the tribes of the earth" will recognize The Prophecy Man. Even though most are not believers, still they will know instinctively. *It's Him! It's Jesus! The Christians were right!* Then *"they will see the Son of Man coming on the clouds with power and great glory."*

Unfortunately, the majority will be caught unprepared. So instead of rejoicing as they see Him return, *"all the tribes of the earth will mourn."* To "mourn" means to be overwhelmingly sad. They will cry out, weep, and wail because their wild, ungodly partying days are over. The clock has officially run out. The game of life is finished. Tragically, they are losers, not winners.

But not everyone will be downcast and terrified. No, no. On the great Day of the Lord, there will be a sizable group of true believers who have been longing for, waiting for, and watching for what Paul called *"the blessed hope"*

(Tit. 2:13). For them, the blasting of the Trumpet of the Ages will be a most welcome sound, as it is written:

> *And He will send His angels with **a great sound of a trumpet**, and they will gather together His elect from the four winds, from one end of heaven to the other* (Matthew 24:31).

"His elect" are those who have believed in Him, loved Him, stood up for Him, and by His grace obeyed His words through thick and thin. Holy angels will *"gather together"* those faithful ones *"from the four winds, from one end of heaven to the other."* Whether they lived in North or South America, Europe, New Zealand, Russia, China, or on islands in the sea (or wherever else), they will be lovingly gathered by myriads of unfallen, holy beings and brought to their Savior, Lord, and King.

Oh, what a day that will be! The Prophecy Man will then have fulfilled His own prediction, "I will come again." The Stone which King Nebuchadnezzar beheld in his mysterious dream will have finally arrived to crush all other opposing kingdoms, *"and it shall stand forever"* (Dan. 2:44). "The sign" the disciples asked about will have been revealed to "all the tribes of the earth."

As Jesus Himself said, *"Then shall the end come"* (Matt. 24:14 KJV).

Yet this book you are now reading is far from over. Are other signs happening now that tell us that we are getting closer to Armageddon? In most levels of professional American football, a designated official sounds a two-minute warning to alert players *that the clock will run out soon.*

Is the clock of fallen human history about to run out?

Have we entered the apocalyptic two-minute warning period?

Keep reading. You are about to discover the answer to that question.

CHAPTER 5

"THE TIME OF THE END"

> "I know the Bible is inspired because it inspires me."
>
> —Dwight L. Moody
> (1837-1899) American evangelist

In the last chapter of the book of Daniel, a holy angel told God's prophet:

*But you, Daniel, shut up the words, and seal the book until **the time of the end**; many shall run to and fro, and knowledge shall increase* (Daniel 12:4).

This verse should be closely examined. After receiving numerous dreams and visions, Daniel was told to "shut up the words" and "seal the book." The "words" referred to are the words of God—communicated through angels—which were given to Daniel in dreams and visions. These words were eventually written down to become the book of Daniel itself. Both the words and the book were to be shut up and sealed, which means that some of these prophecies would not be fully understood "until the time of the end." In the time of the end, the book of Daniel and its end-time prophecies would be unsealed, opened, and unlocked for all the world to see.

When that time finally comes, *"many shall run to and fro, and knowledge shall increase."* The phrase "many shall run to and fro" doesn't mean that people will literally run or sprint on roads or around neighborhoods, sweating profusely, becoming exhausted. Rather, it refers to *the eyes* of men, women, and even children darting back and forth from one Bible verse to another, and from one Bible chapter to another, as they read the words of the Lord that had previously been sealed. Here's a parallel verse that makes this clearer:

> **For the eyes of the Lord run to and fro throughout the whole earth**, to show Himself strong on behalf of those whose heart is loyal to Him (2 Chronicles 16:9).

Here it is "the eyes of the Lord" that "run to and fro." Comparing Scripture with Scripture, we discover that in Daniel 12:4 the angel meant that as the eyes of men, women, and children dart back and forth over the words of God that have previously been locked up and sealed, something wonderful happens—*"knowledge shall increase."* The reason knowledge increases is because in "the time of the end" increasing numbers of humans will have the unprecedented opportunity—previously unavailable to former generations—*to read for themselves and to understand the words of God.*

"The time of the end" is *not the end of the world* but rather refers to a unique time period *before the end,* leading up to it. It's also a time when millions of searching souls are given an unprecedented opportunity to learn the Word of God, which will help them prepare for "the end." In Daniel 12:4, the stated sign that we have entered "the time of the end" is that "many shall run to and fro, and knowledge shall increase." Those three words—*knowledge shall increase*—are about to lead us into an amazing journey.

From the days of *"Adam to Moses"* (Rom. 5:14), God communicated with humans through direct revelations that were then verbally passed down from generation to generation. None of those revelations—as far as we know—were written down. Thus, in those ancient days there was no such thing as a Bible. After God called Moses to be His prophet and to bring Israel out of Egypt (see Exod. 1–4), He later led Moses to write the history of Creation Week, the Fall, Noah and the Flood, and many other events that we can now read about in the first five books of the Bible—Genesis, Exodus, Leviticus, Numbers, and Deuteronomy.

God later inspired different prophets and Bible writers to fill out what is referred to as the Old Testament. After the long-awaited appearance of the Messiah, the Holy Spirit also led Matthew, Mark, Luke, Peter, James, Paul, and Jude to record the critical events in the life of Jesus Christ and of His early Church. The last Bible writer, John, whose writings include the book of Revelation, brought an end to what has become the New Testament.

Moses started writing around 1400 B.C., and John finished his writings around A.D. 96. Thus, the total period of Bible writing was about 1,500 years. Yet throughout that entire time there were no printing presses or copy machines or any of the hi-tech gadgets we now have today. Thus, every page of the Bible (or parts of the Bible) was painstakingly copied—word for word, line by line, book by book—by human hands.

It was a very slow and careful process.

Thus, for a long, long time—for most of human history—there were not many Bibles in existence. During some periods, such as during the Dark Ages, there were only a few copies of God's Book anywhere on earth. Not only that, but many people couldn't read anyway, so even if they happened to obtain a copy or portion of God's Word, to them it was largely "sealed" or locked up. Plus, to purchase a Bible was expensive. Few people ever actually set their eyes on an entire Bible. And if they did, it probably didn't belong to them, or it was locked up in a language they couldn't understand, so they couldn't read it.

Such a state continued until around A.D. 1440 when a German businessman, Johannes Gutenberg, invented the printing press with movable type. Can you guess what was the first book Mr. Gutenberg printed? *It was a Bible.* Due to this history-altering invention, slowly but surely copies of God's sacred Word began to multiply, and the process of translating the Bible into different languages also increased.

Still, for hundreds of years progress was slow. Then, in the late 1700s and early 1800s, things sped up exponentially through the formation of British, European, and American Bible societies wholly dedicated to translating, publishing, and distributing affordable copies of God's Book. Since then, the sacred work of bringing Bibles to the masses has steadily advanced.

On second thought, *advanced* is too tame a word.

Soared is more accurate.

A 2017 article entitled "29 Good Bible Sales Statistics" highlights these salient points:

- By far the most widely translated, purchased, and widely distributed book in all of history is the Bible.

- Between 1815 and 1975, it was estimated that there could have been 5 billion Bibles printed.

- There are more than 168,000 Bibles sold or given away in the United States every day.

- Approximately 20 million Bibles are sold each year in the United States. That's more than double the amount that was sold annually in the 1950s.

- Gideon's International distributed 59,460,000 Bibles worldwide in 2016. That's more than 100 Bibles per minute.

- Zondervan, one of the world's leading Bible publishers, has more than 350 different versions of the Bible that are in print right now.

- 92% of Americans own at least 1 Bible. Two-thirds of those who own a Bible, regardless of religious affiliation, say that the Bible holds the meaning of life.

- The average American Christian owns nine Bibles and wants to purchase more. For this reason, the Bible is excluded from book bestseller lists because it would always be on top.

- 1,300 translations of the Bible are in new languages.

- More than 2,100 languages now have the Bible (or a portion of it) available in those languages.

- The annual sales of all versions of the Bible routinely tops $425 million.

- Over 100 million Bibles are printed every year.

- In the week after the September 11, 2001 attacks in the US, some retailers saw 40% increases in Bible sales.

- In 2005, Thomas Nelson, another leading Bible publisher, was sold for $473 million. They publish 60 different editions of the Bible.

- In the world today, there are more than 80,000 different versions of the Bible.

- Estimated total sales of Bibles has now topped *six billion.*[1]

Six billion Bibles sold! Quite impressive, don't you think? But there's more. As we all know, in recent years the world has gone increasingly digital. As never before, hi-tech is in. Here are a few more statistics from the same article referenced above:

- YouVersion, a top downloaded Bible app for mobile devices, has over 100 million total downloads and counting. It's also been one of the top 100 free apps for 3 consecutive years.

- More than 66,000 people are using a Bible app at any given second.

- 77% of people say that they read the Bible more frequently because they have it available on a mobile device.

- Two-thirds of people prefer Bible apps because it gives them access to multiple versions of the Bible without the added cost.[2]

"You've come a long way, baby!" was an advertising slogan first used in 1968 to promote Virginia Slims cigarettes. While the product is totally different, the principle surely applies to the worldwide distribution of God's Book. It's come a long, long, long way. Remember, for the vast bulk of human history, very few people had access to, had ever looked upon, or were privileged to own and read a copy of the Bible.

But everything has changed.

And in the last few years, it has changed *dramatically*.

What's going on? Is there any prophetic significance to this? No doubt there is. Approximately 500 years before Jesus was even born, a holy angel told Daniel:

> *But you, Daniel, shut up the words, and seal the book until **the time of the end**; many shall run to and fro, and knowledge shall increase* (Daniel 12:4).

To my readers I say—Bible prophecy is being *fulfilled* before our very eyes. The words of God recorded in Daniel's book (and in other Bible books) are now unlocked, unsealed, and are easily accessible for human eyes to read like never before.

Just take your smartphone and download a Bible app. It's free. Or download other apps, such as Bible Hub, which gives you instant access to many translations, Strong's Concordance, Hebrew and Greek definitions, and Bible commentaries. While most humans don't realize it, this simple fact is a key biblical sign that we have entered the time of the end.

"Knowledge shall increase," declared God's angel. But as we all know, this increase of knowledge doesn't only apply to the Holy Scriptures. On November 23, 2018, an

op-ed entitled, "Knowledge doubles almost every day, and it's set to increase," was published online by the Digital Journal. In that article, Feras A. Batarseh of the London School of Economics points out:

> Until year 1900, human knowledge approximately doubled every century. However, by 1950 human knowledge doubled every 25 years. In 2000, human knowledge would double every year. Now, our knowledge is *almost doubling every day.*[3]

The Digital Journal even referred to the "knowledge tsunami" we are all so familiar with. If the early American hero Daniel Boone (1734–1820) could somehow be transported into our hi-tech times, he would probably be so shocked that his rifle might go off and shoot himself in the foot! Mega-cities, towering skyscrapers, superfast flying machines, international satellites and space stations, hands-free electric cars, underground transportation systems, fiber optics, facial recognition security devices, iPhones, and instant messaging—these are just a few current wonders.

What will come tomorrow?

No one knows.

The truth is that the increase of knowledge *generally* has contributed to the availability of biblical knowledge *specifically.* The two are closely related—and both should be viewed as fulfillments of prophecy. Yet the Digital Journal's article also correctly states that "This additional knowledge does not necessarily mean we are becoming wiser."

How true this is.

Having instant access to God's Book, Bible apps, and multiple translations isn't enough for a true knowledge of God's words to *increase*—which is the primary focus of Daniel 12:4. For that to happen, we need humble hearts, a sincere desire for truth, a willingness to repent (to turn from sin), and an openness to the deep moving of *"the Spirit of truth"* whom Jesus said will guide us *"into all truth"* (John 16:13). Ultimately, we need a true *"knowledge of our Lord and Savior Jesus Christ"* (2 Pet. 3:18), which includes a knowledge of His infinite love, sacrifice for our sins, tender mercy, life-changing forgiveness, and saving grace.

After speaking to the prophet Daniel, the angel of God continued by saying:

Go your way, Daniel, for the words are closed up and sealed till the time of the end. Many shall be purified, made white, and refined, but the wicked shall do wickedly; and none of the wicked shall understand, but the wise shall understand (Daniel 12:9-10).

When Daniel 12:4 and Daniel 12:9-10 are knit together, it becomes clear that God's ultimate plan is that in the time of the end, when a knowledge of His words shall increase, such knowledge shall draw, impress, convict, cleanse, and purify human hearts from sin, selfishness, and falsehood. *"Many shall be purified, made white, and refined,"* said the angel. Yet sadly, because multitudes today are so mesmerized by Hollywood lights, hi-tech gadgets, and life's insane busyness, they are missing life's true purpose, blessings, and opportunities.

Slow down. Stop. Think. Look around. Open the eyes of your heart. The evidence is overwhelming. Surely, the long-awaited, biblically predicted "time of the end" has arrived. This also tells us that silently, stealthily, and mostly unnoticed, the return of Jesus *"as a thief"* is getting closer (Rev. 16:15). Someday soon—none know how soon—the battle of Armageddon will be fought.

"None of the wicked shall understand," said a holy angel sent from God, *"but the wise shall understand"* (Dan. 12:10).

Let's be among the wise.

NOTES

1. Brandon Gaille, "27 Good Bible Sales Statistics," May 23, 2017, https://brandongaille.com/27-good-bible-sales -statistics.

2. Ibid.

3. Tim Sandle, "Op-Ed: Knowledge doubles almost every day, and it's set to increase," Digital Journal, November 23, 2018, http://www.digitaljournal.com/tech-and-science/ science/op-ed-knowledge-doubles-almost-every-day-and -it-s-set-to-increase/article/537543.

CHAPTER 6

"THERE SHALL BE SIGNS"

"Sometimes one misses the sign posts as you're going down the road. They aren't as obvious as they become when you get to the end of the road."

—Leon Russell, American musician[1]

As we've already seen, a few days before Jesus was unjustly delivered over to Roman soldiers to be publicly scourged and crucified, His disciples asked Him this loaded question:

What will be the sign of Your coming, and of the end of the age? (Matthew 24:3)

Christ's lengthy answer starts in the next verse (Matt. 24:4) and continues all the way to the end of Matthew

25. With slight variations, the book of Mark records His response to the same question in Mark 13:1-37, as does Luke in Luke 21:8-36.

"There will be signs" declared the greatest Teacher the world has ever seen (Luke 21:25).

An important clarification is in order. It is surely true that many of the signs Jesus mentioned are not new. In fact, a host of them—such as earthquakes, wars, and the emergence of false messiahs—did occur prior to A.D. 70 when Jerusalem and its temple were demolished by Roman legions. Beyond A.D. 70, it is also true that many of these same signs have been occurring off and on throughout the last two thousand years. Yet some of the signs are wholly unique to the end times, as we shall soon see.

Rest assured that in this book I will not set any dates, for Jesus Himself clarified, *"But of that day and hour no one knows, not even the angels of heaven, but My Father only"* (Matt. 24:36). On the other hand, He also said:

> *Now learn this parable from the fig tree: When its branch has already become tender and puts forth leaves, you know that summer is near. So you also, when you see all these things,* ***know that it is near—at the doors!*** (Matthew 24:32-33)

When the disciples saw *"Jerusalem surrounded by armies"* in A.D. 66, they were to *"know that its desolation [was] near"* (Luke 21:20). It's the same with the end times. As we approach Armageddon, there will once again be a cluster of signs that should speak to our hearts, too, like the leafing out of fig trees after winter indicating that *"summer is near."* When we *"see all these things,"* we too can *"know that it is near—at the doors!"* If we ignore such signs, like the Jewish rulers did before A.D. 70, the result will be catastrophic. But if we are awake and alert, we have nothing to fear.

Some of my readers may be able to relate to a simple story. Did you ever sit on a railroad track as a child, waiting for a train to come into view? Excitedly, you wait and listen. Long before the train arrives, you place your ear on the smooth surface of the rail and wait to feel the faintest vibration. The first tremor is almost indiscernible. You wonder if it's just your imagination; but then, you are certain the faint vibration means the train is approaching. After a few moments, the sound in your ear becomes more distinct, gradually getting louder with each passing second.

You glance up, half-expecting the train to roll around the corner—but not yet.

Still, no train.

But soon there is a new development. You now hear the sound of the train itself, which joins the vibration on the track. Then, finally, you see the large, imposing locomotive engine come into view. As your heart thrills with excitement, the noise quickly becomes a deafening roar as the massive train rushes right past you just a few feet away.

Similarly, we too can catch *the gradually increasing sounds* of an approaching end of the world. However, only those who are intently listening for the steady tread of events will *"know that it is near—at the doors!"* Tragically, many have died at railroad crossings because they weren't paying attention, or perhaps they had turned up the radio in their car so loud that it drowned out the warning blast from the oncoming locomotive. In Matthew 24, Mark 13, and in Luke 21, Jesus gave the world certain signs of His approaching return; yet today, most are ignoring these critical apocalyptic indicators. Many are so absorbed in *"carousing, drunkenness, and cares of this life"* that they don't even hear the warning blasts (Luke 21:34).

All the while, the train is getting closer.

If we're not ready, soon it will be too late.

Here's another simple illustration many more of you can probably relate to—having a baby. Notice carefully what Paul wrote:

*But concerning the times and the seasons, brethren, you have no need that I should write to you. For you yourselves know perfectly that the day of the Lord so comes as a thief in the night. For when they say, "Peace and safety!" then sudden destruction comes upon them, **as labor pains upon a pregnant woman**. And they shall not escape* (1 Thessalonians 5:1-3).

These verses describe *"the day of the Lord"* when Jesus will return unexpectedly *"as a thief in the night."* While many will dismiss the advance warnings and cry *"peace and safety,"* Paul wrote that *"sudden destruction"* will eventually overwhelm them. Now notice carefully. Such desolation will come *"as labor pains upon a pregnant woman. And they shall not escape"* (1 Thess. 5:3).

The phrase "as labor pains upon a pregnant woman" contains a valuable lesson. When a woman conceives and begins carrying a child, she still has approximately nine months until the day of birth. But as she gets closer to delivery, her labor pains begin. Just a few pangs at first, but then they come faster and faster and faster. Finally, out comes her precious little one.

Now don't miss this point: Paul said it would be similar to the approach of the day of the Lord. Labor pains, or signs, will increase as the Prophesied Day draws near.

Therefore, while it is true that destructive earthquakes, devastating famines, and terrible wars have taken place throughout history, we can also expect such woes to *increase in both frequency and intensity*—like birth pains do—as we draw closer to the day of the Lord. Paul also wrote:

For we know that the whole creation groans and labors with birth pangs together until now (Romans 8:22).

Here Paul connects birth pangs with the groaning of God's whole creation. Putting two and two together, we can expect that the labor pains that precede Jesus Christ's return as a thief in the night will involve *increasing and more intense convulsions in nature.* Therefore, especially in *"the time of the end"* (Daniel 12:4), we should expect to see a steady increase of rapid-fire, nature-related, back-to-back catastrophes. Earth itself will groan under a weight of woe. Unfortunately, countless men, women, and even children will also suffer the consequences.

Here's another illustration all travelers are familiar with. As everyone knows, all interstate highways have road signs. When I lived in California, I always passed them on Highway 5 when I drove my car from Sacramento to Los Angeles. As I journeyed on, I was always keen to notice such milestones as "352 miles to Los Angeles," "175 miles to Los Angeles," "52 miles to Los Angeles," and so on. After many weary hours, I eventually rolled into LA.

The same is true of biblical signs for the approaching "end of the world." When we discover what these signs are, and especially when we witness them occurring at the same time, then we can know that we're getting closer to the final, predicted apocalypse.

As you can see, this chapter in *Approaching Armageddon* is called "There Shall Be Signs." My chapter title is taken from the exact words of Jesus in Luke 21:25. Notice carefully what Jesus said:

> **And there shall be signs** *in the sun, and in the moon, and in the stars; and upon the earth distress of nations, with perplexity; the sea and the waves roaring; men's hearts failing them for fear, and for looking after those things which are coming on the earth: for the powers of heaven shall be shaken* (Luke 21:25-26 KJV).

If you do some online research, you will discover that in the past few hundred years, some exceedingly strange things have taken place *"in the sun, and in the moon, and in the stars."* Look up "The Great Dark Day of May 19, 1780," when not only was earth's blazing sun completely darkened at midday, but the moon soon took on the appearance of blood. Or search for, "The Night the Stars Fell on November 12, 1833," when an estimated 240,000 falling stars were visible for approximately 9 hours. You can still read the reports. There is no doubt that those who experienced those stunning events thought they were harbingers of the end of the world. As we advance still closer, we can expect more shocking sights in the atmosphere above our heads.

But what about here on earth?

Jesus continued, *"And upon the earth distress of nations, with perplexity."* Notice that particular word—*distress*. Doesn't it sound like a word we use a lot? Remove the first two letters, and what do you get? *Stress*. It isn't a stretch to say that the words *distress* and *stress* apply more forcibly to present day conditions than at any other previous time in human history. City living, captivating technologies, global pollution, civil unrest, increasing immorality and brutality, the unprecedented busyness of life in the new millennium, natural catastrophes, rampant diseases, plus economic woes—these are all creating daily stresses as never before.

Google the word *stress*, and you will discover a plethora of websites about stress tests, stress seminars, stress relief, stress management, stress disorders, stress institutes, and how-to-lower-stress techniques. In 2008, National Geographic even released a frightening documentary called *Stress: Portrait of a Killer*, which highlights the health dangers from stress threatening this generation.

Nearly two thousand years ago, looking down to the last days, Jesus Christ saw it coming. "On the earth," He predicted, "distress of nations" would prevail. Then He added, "with perplexity." The underlying Greek word for "perplexity" means "finding no solution." In other words, society's rampant problems will eventually become unsolvable.

Sound familiar?

Has the United States government made real progress with its multi-trillion-dollar national debt? No. Has our economy been fixed? No. Have we eliminated the threat of a nuclear holocaust? No. Have we solved our desperate healthcare crisis? No. Have we initiated programs capable of feeding the world's starving millions? No. Have we eliminated racism and crime? No. Have we been able to stem the tide of deadly earthquakes, fires, droughts, floods, tornadoes, and hurricanes that keep pounding planet earth? No. No. No. Truly, the words, "and on the earth distress of nations, with perplexity" accurately describe the daily reports we receive from CNN, ABC, NBC, and Fox News.

It's all happening right now.

Once again, Jesus Christ told the truth.

He continued: *"the sea and the waves roaring"* (Luke 21:25). The oceans themselves have become a rising threat. On Friday, March 11, 2011, one of the five most powerful earthquakes ever recorded, registering 9.0 on the Richter scale, struck off the coast of Japan, triggering a series of deadly tsunamis, one as tall as 133 feet. When "the sea and the waves" stopped "roaring," not only were more than fifteen thousand people dead and three nuclear reactors crippled, but planet Earth itself had shifted on its axis!

Newsweek commented:

> The quake, the tsunami, and the meltdown at the Fukushima nuclear-power plant in Japan are cautionary examples suggesting what could happen in the United States, but there are plausible scenarios in America that are worse. Much worse.[2]

Much worse?

I hate to say it, but the popular phrase, "You ain't seen nothing yet," applies. Without skipping a beat, Jesus continued, *"men's hearts failing them from fear"* (Luke 21:26). What is the number one cause of death in developed countries, including the United States? It's cardiovascular disease. Or, more simply, heart disease. Highly processed fatty foods pose a serious threat to us all. "The first symptom many people feel that they are having a heart attack," one doctor commented, "is sudden death." Jesus also added another word as a contributing cause—*fear*. Talk to your doctor. Chronic fear, stress, and nervousness can raise blood cholesterol levels and blood pressure, leading to heart attacks.

Yet Christ's words imply much more. Look again closely: *"Men's hearts failing them for fear, **and for looking after those things which are coming on the earth**."* The main reason Jesus gives as to why human hearts will fail them from fear is because they are *"looking after those things which are coming on the earth"* (Luke 21:26 KJV). This verse is uncanny. Think about it. Jesus said this nearly two thousand years ago; yet today it is now possible for people all around the globe—in ways unknown to previous generations—to literally *look* at *"those things which are coming on the earth."*

How?

On TV, on the internet, and on YouTube.

Unlike what occurred on a limited scope in A.D. 70 when Jerusalem was sacked by Romans, the context of this specific prediction is *a global mess.* "Upon the earth distress of *nations*," said the Lord. In A.D. 70, technology had not developed enough for people all over planet Earth to be *"looking after those things that are coming upon the earth."*

But now it has.

I repeat: *now* it has.

Our situation is truly unlike what has been possible for the majority of human history.

The last part of verse 26 adds, *"for the powers of the heavens will be shaken."* This implies that as we near the sunset of fallen human history our solar system itself will do bizarre things.

Imagine with me. Let's say a gigantic asteroid suddenly headed our way (in the last few years this has happened many times). Because of NASA, sophisticated telescopes, TV, the internet, and YouTube, billions of viewers could literally witness real-time images of an approaching fireball long before disaster struck. The same is true of a whole host of possible crises. Because of developing technologies, anything that seriously threatens humanity's collective global sanity can be watched almost instantly.

This is all a direct fulfillment of Bible prophecy. As never before, we are the *looking* generation, exactly as Jesus said.

What's next on the horizon? Brace yourself. Jesus continued, *"Then they will see the Son of Man coming in a cloud with power and great glory"* (Luke 21:27).

The Truth Teller said it. According to the Man who doesn't lie, it won't be too long after earth's inhabitants have been fearfully "looking after those things which are coming on the earth" that there will be a major scene change. Then will come the final act of earth's drama. The curtain will drop. The buzzer will sound. Game over.

> *Then they will **see** the Son of Man coming in a cloud with power and great glory. Now when these things begin to happen, look up and lift up your heads, **because your redemption draws near** (Luke 21:27-28).*

This prediction also once again clarifies exactly what "the end of the world" really means. There's no need to guess. It won't come because a global climate emergency has caused humanity's demise. Or the detonation of a terrorist nuclear device. Or an EMP. Or an uncontrollable pandemic that wipes out every human. Or another ice age supposedly caused by crashing asteroids. Or an evil alien attack like Hollywood portrayed in its blockbuster movie, *Independence Day*. No, no. According to Jesus Christ, the end will come when He, Himself—the Son of Man—personally descends from heavenly skies in *"a cloud with power and great glory"* attended by an innumerable company of holy angels.

No matter what some teach, this didn't happen in A.D. 70.

But it's coming.

That's exactly what Jesus said.

NOTE

1. Mike Ragogna, "Life Journeys: Conversations With Leon Russell, Judy Collins and John Gorka," Huffpost.com, March 31, 2013, https://www.huffpost.com/entry/life -journeys-conversatio_b_5062965.

2. Christopher Dickey, "Time to Brace for the Next 9/11," Newsweek.com, September 4, 2011, https://www .newsweek.com/time-brace-next-911-67389.

CHAPTER 7

"NEAR—AT THE DOOR!"

"There's a great deal in the Bible about the signs we're to watch for, and when these signs all converge at one place we can be sure that we're close to the end of the age."

—Billy Graham (1918-2018) American evangelist, spiritual advisor to 12 US presidents

From 1975 to 1977, I was a student at North Hollywood High School in Southern California. Basketball was my favorite sport, and I was accepted as a player on our school basketball team. During one particular game in the gymnasium, perhaps I was overly aggressive. Our team won. As was our usual practice at the end of each game, our players cordially shook hands with the other team.

But when I reached out my hand to shake hands with one of the other players...

Pow!

His fist punched me in the face!

I found out later that my attacker's name was John Naviera. John and I had never met before, but during that game I must have irritated him somehow. So at the end of the game, he let me have it. Looking back, I don't remember all the details of how our conflict was resolved, but I do know that John and I eventually became best friends. We played basketball together, went camping together near Lake Tahoe, and did lots of other things together.

It all started with a fist.

Then, we became friends.

I decided to relay this simple story because some of the details in this chapter may seem like a punch to your face, too. But I want to assure you that I mean you no harm, and I also hope that when you finish reading this chapter and this book you will realize the truth of this biblical proverb:

Faithful are the wounds of a friend, but the kisses of an enemy are deceitful (Proverbs 27:6).

As we've already seen, in the pages of the Holy Bible, there are numerous signs listed that are indicative that we are fast *Approaching Armageddon.* I've covered a few of them so far. Now it's time to list many more. As you will see, these signs are nothing like the sensational (and mostly fictional) omens that appear daily on the covers of America's sensational tabloids. By contrast, here is a genuine list of bona fide, sober biblical signs worth listing.

FALSE PROPHETS, FALSE MESSIAHS

Immediately after His disciples' question, "What will be the sign of Your coming, and of the end of the age?" the Bible reports:

Jesus answered and said to them: "Take heed that no one deceives you. For many will come in My name, saying, 'I am the Christ,' and will deceive many" (Matthew 24:4-5).

Many false prophets will rise up and deceive many (Matthew 24:11).

Then if anyone says to you, "Look, here is the Christ!" or "There!" do not believe it. For false christs and false prophets will rise and show great signs and wonders to deceive, if possible, even the elect. See, I have told you beforehand (Matthew 24:23-25).

It's true that false prophets, false teachers, and false messiahs have appeared throughout history, but we can expect them to be especially prolific (and deceptive) in the time of the end. Today, many of these false teachers have vast numbers of followers.

"This man claims he is Jesus Christ reincarnated," ran a *National Geographic* headline published on July 12, 2017 about a self-proclaimed messiah in Brazil.[1] "While Álvaro Theiss was fasting, he came to believe that he was Jesus Christ reborn." At the time of this article, Mr. Theiss had 12 chosen disciples, and lived on a compound he called, "The New Jerusalem." "[Theiss] regularly preaches on YouTube and on Facebook Live, on which he has over 330,000 followers. ...His story, along with profiles of four other self-proclaimed messiahs, appear in the August [2017] issue of *National Geographic* magazine."[2]

Another example is Pastor Apollo Quiboloy in the Philippines, founder of "the Kingdom of Jesus Christ The Name That Is Above Every Name." His website (as of July 2020) says he has "7 million followers worldwide and growing—covering 200 countries and 2000 cities, spanning most continents of the world."[3] Just a few of his teachings are:

Pastor Apollo Quiboloy was the first man to be called by the Almighty Father to the true and genuine repentance. He was the first man to have endured all the fiery trials of persecution and hardship and to have overcome them all without breaking his covenant with the Father. He was the first man to finally eject the serpent seed, breaking the chain of sin by his absolute obedience to the Father's will. ... the Almighty Father anointed him and made him His Appointed Son in these last days.

...The Second Coming is happening in millions of sons and daughters of the Father in the Kingdom Nation of God on earth today, beginning with the Appointed Son of God, as the firstborn, Pastor Apollo C. Quiboloy.

...He has become the Inheritor of all things—the Sonship and dominion that was promised to Adam in the beginning. He is the Almighty Father's Representative on this earth today.[4]

Really? "Take heed that no one deceives you," warned Jesus. How can we detect a deceiver in disguise? If a person claims to be the Son of God Himself, that's a clear sign of delusion. Others don't make such blatant claims, and some may actually claim to believe in Jesus, but their words and actions deny their faith.

What if they perform actual miracles? Wouldn't that be a sure indication they have been sent by God? Not according to Jesus. Don't be fooled. Jesus said many *"false christs"* and *"false prophets"* will perform *"great signs and wonders."* Yet beneath such miracles lurk demonic forces seeking *"to deceive, if possible, even the elect"* (Matt. 24:24). Don't fall for these tricksters. The only safe path is to closely follow *the real Jesus* and to hold firmly to what He actually says *in His Holy Word.*

WARS, NATION AGAINST NATION

Next, Jesus declared:

And you will hear of wars and rumors of wars. See that you are not troubled; for all these things must come to pass, but the end is not yet. For nation will rise against nation, and kingdom against kingdom (Matthew 24:6-7).

Conflicts, violent revolutions, bloody battles, and awful wars aren't new, but we can expect them to increase in scope and destructiveness in these end times. Our most recent 20th century witnessed World War I, World War II, the Korean War, the Vietnam War, the Persian Gulf War, and other wars. Weapons of destruction have also become much more deadly, such as the devastating nuclear bombs dropped on Hiroshima and Nagasaki in 1945.

If King Nebuchadnezzar, Alexander the Great, Julius Caesar, or Napoleon could somehow witness the detonation of those nukes, they would hardly believe what they were seeing. I imagine it would be the same for any of us, too. Such scenes are almost unimaginable.

During "the full twentieth century," wrote Milton Leitenberg of Cornell University, "approximately 231 million people died in wars and conflicts."[5] The advanced weaponry available today is unprecedented. Through further developments in technology, watchers can even keep track of how many wars and conflicts are raging at this exact moment. Wikipedia's article, "List of ongoing armed conflicts" is available for those who have an interest to read such things. Personally, I'm not obsessed with those details. It's enough for me to know that Jesus predicted such things, and that when they happen there is hope beyond the bullets.

FAMINES, PESTILENCES, EARTHQUAKES

Jesus continued:

And there will be famines, pestilences, and earth-quakes in various places (Matthew 24:7).

Once again, these aren't new. And again, Wikipedia is helpful. If you read its article, "List of Famines," you can easily scroll down through a sequence of historical famines starting at around 2000 B.C. up to the present. It also should be clear by now that—in contrast to fiction, speculation, and mythology—biblical predictions aren't fanciful, but are absolutely real.

> Every year, around 9 million people die of hunger, according to the international relief agency Mercy Corps. That's more than the death toll of AIDS, malaria and tuberculosis combined.[6]

Famines are horrific, especially when small children suffer. Just to clarify, just because Jesus predicted these things, God is in no wise responsible for such nightmares. He weeps, too. They are all the result of sin running its course until the Day when He finally acts to rid His earth of such terrors.

More on that soon.

The word *pestilence* means diseases. Once again, history has had its share of them. The website of MPH Online provides an excellent resource for students seeking master's degrees in public health. One of their articles, "Outbreak: 10 of the Worst Pandemics in History," reveals not only the worst pandemics, but estimated death tolls.[7] Here are just some of them:

- Antonine Plague (A.D. 165)—death toll: 5 million
- Plague of Justinian (541-542)—death toll: 25 million
- The Black Death (1346–1353)—death toll: 75-200 million
- Third Cholera Pandemic (1852–1860)—death toll: 1 million
- Flu Pandemic (1918)—death toll: 20-50 million
- Asian Flu (1956–1958)—death toll: 2 million
- HIV/AIDS Pandemic (at its peak, 2005–2012)—death toll: 36 million

As everyone knows today, in December of 2019 the novel coronavirus, which originated in Wuhan, China, began wreaking havoc around the world within a few short months. MPH Online reports:

The WHO declared Covid-19 a pandemic in March [of 2020], and by the end of that month, the world saw more than a half-million people infected and nearly 30,000 deaths. The infection rate in the US and other nations was still spiking.

With the coronavirus pandemic, people all over the world have become more aware of the best practices during a pandemic, from careful hand-washing to social distancing. Countries across the world declared mandatory stay-at-home measures, closing schools, businesses, and public places. Dozens of companies and many more independent researchers began working on tests, treatments, and vaccines. *The push for the human race to survive the pandemic became the primary concern in the world.*[8]

The COVID-19 crisis has created endless controversies. At the time of this writing, the current numbers are approximately 20 million infections and nearly 800,000 deaths worldwide. Whether these figures are truly accurate or not, and how long this pandemic will last, is anyone's guess. But there is one thing we can be sure of. Jesus Christ declared that "pestilences" would come, and the deadly novel coronavirus is definitely part of the fulfillment of His prediction.

Jesus added, *"There will be great earthquakes in various places"* (Luke 21:11). Nothing is certain these days. Even the ground beneath our feet often shakes, sometimes resulting in tremendous damage and loss of life. While it is surely true that earthquakes have occurred throughout history, we can expect more large ones in the days ahead. We can also expect many other nature-based disasters like violent storms and hurricanes, raging floods, bellowing volcanic eruptions, and fierce fires.

The Old Testament prophet Joel also predicted:

*And it shall come to pass in the last days, says God...I will show wonders in heaven above and **signs** in the earth beneath: blood and fire and vapor of smoke. The sun shall be turned into darkness, and the moon into blood, before the coming of the great and awesome day of the Lord* (Acts 2:17-20).

INCREASING LAWLESSNESS

In *Approaching Armageddon,* I won't comment on every prediction Jesus made; but I will highlight many of them. Here's another one:

> *And because lawlessness will abound, the love of many will grow cold* (Matthew 24:12).

In this verse, the King James Version uses the word *iniquity,* whereas the New King James Version (quoted above) uses *lawlessness.* The original Greek word is *anomian* which, according to Strong's Lexicon, literally means "lawlessness, disobedience, sin." The underlying root word is *anomos,* which means "violation of law or wickedness." Jesus said lawlessness would abound—which comes from the Greek word, *plethynthenai,* meaning "to increase or multiply."

In a nutshell, Jesus meant that sin, which is the violation of God's holy Ten Commandment law (see Exod. 20:1-20; Rom. 3:20; 7:7; 1 John 3:4; James 2:8-12), will keep growing like weeds taking over a garden. The result? *"The love of many will grow cold."* Have you heard of global warming? Here Jesus refers to a different trend, which I call *global cooling.* In other words, as we get closer to His return, real love, God's love, moral love, will abysmally decline.

Highly paid musicians today often sing about love, but all too often it's merely a shallow, mushy, Hollywood type of love that lacks moral substance. God's love is totally different. Paul wrote:

But God demonstrates His own love toward us, in that while we were still sinners, Christ died for us. Much more then, having now been justified by His blood, we shall be saved from wrath through Him (Romans 5:8-9).

Sin is serious—more serious than any of us realize. After indulging in it, Adam and Eve were shut out of Paradise (see Gen. 3). In fact, sin is so serious that, in order to reopen those gates for us, God's own Son had to become human so He could bear our sins and pay an awful price— the divine death penalty. *"Christ died for us,"* meaning on our behalf. When we finally grasp the depth of His love, repent, and trust the merits of His blood, we are then justified, which means we are legally accounted just or not guilty in the sight of God. Thus, we shall be saved from the just wrath of a holy God that will someday fall upon all unrepentant sinners.

Because of false prophets, false teachers, and satanic delusions, most people today have no clue about these truths. Because of false views of love, sin just keeps multiplying like malignant cancer cells in a body. Tragically, in most human hearts true love is dying out. Just look around. This evil trend is evident on all sides. But Jesus Christ is still a fountain of mercy and compassion for all who are willing to surrender to His love and grace.

We all need that love!

And it is fully available—no matter who we are or what we've done.

CORRUPTION AND VIOLENCE AS IN THE DAYS OF NOAH

Moving further down in His message recorded in Matthew 24, Jesus also predicted:

But as the days of Noah were, so also will the coming of the Son of Man be. For as in the days before the flood, they were eating and drinking, marrying and giving in marriage, until the day that Noah entered the ark, and did not know until the flood came and took them all away, so also will the coming of the Son of Man be (Matthew 24:37-39).

What was it like in Noah's day? The Bible reports:

Then the Lord saw that the wickedness of man was great in the earth, and that every intent of the thoughts of his heart was only evil continually.

The earth also was corrupt before God, and the earth was filled with violence. So God looked upon the earth, and indeed it was corrupt; for all flesh had corrupted their way on the earth.

And God said to Noah, "The end of all flesh has come before Me, for the earth is filled with violence through them; and behold, I will destroy them with the earth" (Genesis 6:5,11-13).

In those long-ago days described in the first book of the Holy Bible, human waywardness finally became so awful that God couldn't tolerate it any longer. Three descriptive words for the widespread immorality were *wickedness*, *corruption*, and *violence*.

Do we see such things today? No doubt, especially in U.S. cities like Chicago, Detroit, New York, Saint Louis, and Los Angeles. Other cities particularly known for violent crime include Tijuana, Mexico and Natal, Brazil. As we approach Armageddon, we can expect racial tensions, brutality, rioting, mayhem, madness, and pandemonium to increase in many cities worldwide.

Highly organized, brutal street gangs like MS-13, the Latin Kings, Crips, Bloods, 18th Street Gang, and countless others perform acts too cruel to mention. Then there are the drug traffickers, sex traffickers, and child-porn traffickers whose corruptions make the heart sick. Then there are radical, anarchist activities from violent organizations like Antifa, plus the sinister plots of radical Islamic terrorist groups. It is not the purpose of this book to delve into graphic, gory details, but you get the idea.

If this isn't enough, there's also the steady stream of violence that regularly beams into the heads and hearts of young and old through media, including scores of violent video games like *Grand Theft Auto V,* which includes sexual violence against women and torture. A 2002 report entitled, "Media violence: advice for parents," published by the National Institute of Health, declares:

> By the time they reach age 18, American children will have seen 16,000 simulated murders and 200,000 acts of violence (American Psychiatric Association, 1998). Media violence can be hazardous to children's health, and studies point overwhelmingly to a causal connection between media violence and aggressive attitudes, values and behaviors in some children (Congressional

Public Health Summit, 2000). Through education in clinics, schools, and primary care offices, pediatric nurses can minimize the impact of media violence. They can obtain comprehensive media histories on children and families. They can teach children and parents about the effects of media violence and advise them how to avoid exposure. Nurses can also encourage the entertainment industry to exercise more responsibility in the ways they entertain children.[9]

That report came out in 2002.

Today, it just keeps getting worse.

And above and beyond all this violence, we can add the unspeakable horror of countless innocent babies whose lives have been tragically terminated before they were even born. Approximately 56 million abortions are performed each year in the world, reports the World Health Organization.[10]

For biblical evidence that God considers the unborn to be fully human, read Psalm 139:14; Jeremiah 1:5; and Luke 1:41-44. To learn more about this nightmare; its terrible effects on fathers, mothers, and families; and how

God still offers love, grace, and forgiveness to post-abortive women, watch White Horse Media's 13-part series, *The Abortion Controversy: Two Women Tell Their Stories of Hope and Healing.*

Again, I realize that unjust acts against the innocent aren't new and that violence has been perpetrated on earth for a long, long time. Yet finally, in the days of Noah, enough was enough. It was time for The moral Governor of the Universe to act in just judgment. It was time for rain. Not just a few drops, but a torrential downpour mercifully sent to wash the earth from its insane moral pollution.

After 120 years of planning, sawing, hammering, building, preaching, and pleading, God finally commanded Noah to enter the safety of the ark. His family followed. Then suddenly, an invisible hand closed the massive door as *"the Lord shut him in"* (Gen. 7:16). The world didn't expect anything to happen next. "A global flood is impossible!" claimed so-called scientists and experts. "Noah is a crazy old fool!"

But something *did* happen.

Jesus said that the mocking multitudes *"did not know until the flood came and took them all away"* (Matt. 24:39).

Was there really a global flood? Intelligent design researchers, geologists, and scientists think so, seeing plenty of supporting evidence in the structure of the geologic column and the fossil record that points to sudden and catastrophic water action worldwide.

To strengthen your faith, read *A Flood of Evidence: 40 Reasons Noah and the Flood Still Matter* co-authored by the president and founder of "Answers in Genesis" Ken Ham, along with Bodie Hodge.[11]

Just look at the Grand Canyon in Colorado, which was clearly carved out by unmeasurable torrents of water.

The silent evidence is in its rocks.

Notice carefully. After saying, *"the flood came and took them all away,"* Jesus added: ***"so also will the coming of the Son of Man be"*** (Matt. 24:39).

SEXUAL SINS AS IN THE DAYS OF LOT

Along similar lines, Jesus also warned:

Likewise as it was also in the days of Lot: They ate, they drank, they bought, they sold, they planted, they built; but on the day that Lot went out of Sodom it rained fire and brimstone from heaven and destroyed them all. Even so will it be in the day when the Son of Man is revealed (Luke 17:28-30).

What was it like in Lot's day? What was it that led our merciful Creator to finally incinerate Sodom and Gomorrah? The Holy Bible offers this plain answer:

Even as Sodom and Gomorrha, and the cities about them in like manner, giving themselves over to fornication, and going after strange flesh, are set forth for an example, suffering the vengeance of eternal fire (Jude 7 KJV).

"Fornication" refers to sex outside of marriage. The institution of marriage itself, which originally took place between one man (Adam) and one woman (Eve), revealed the Creator's perfect plan. Notice these wonderful details:

And the Lord God said, "It is not good that man should be alone; I will make him a helper comparable to him."...And the Lord God caused a deep sleep to fall on Adam, and he slept; and He took one of his ribs, and closed up the flesh in its place. Then the rib which the Lord God had taken from man He made into a woman, and He brought her to the man. And Adam said: "This is now bone of my bones and flesh of my flesh; she shall be called Woman, because she was taken out of Man." Therefore a man shall leave his father and mother and be joined to his wife, and

they shall become one flesh. And they were both
naked, the man and his wife, and were not ashamed
(Genesis 2:18,21-25).

In this dawn-of-time passage, the Holy Book identifies the *man*, a *woman*, *father*, and *mother*, showing the
biological distinction between men and women. Notice
also that when a man leaves his father and mother, he is
to be joined to his wife (not to his boyfriend, girlfriend, or
partner), and *"they shall become one flesh,"* which includes
the gift of sexual intercourse that consummates the act
of marriage. Built on this bedrock foundation, fornication
occurs when two people engage in full physical intimacy
outside of biblical marriage.

According to the Holy Scriptures, fornication is a sin.

It is a departure from God's plan.

This was one of the sins of Sodom. But there's more.
Jude added that the inhabitants of Sodom, Gomorrah, and
of nearby cities also indulged in *"going after strange flesh."*
To know what this means, read Genesis 19. Two strang-
ers, who were really holy angels disguised as humans,
showed up one evening at the gate of Sodom. Lot took
them into his house as honored guests; but before they
went to sleep, a riotous crowd surrounded his home.
God's Word reports:

*Now before they lay down, the men of the city, the men of Sodom, both old and young, all the people from every quarter, surrounded the house. And they called to Lot and said to him, "Where are the men who came to you tonight? Bring them out to us **that we may know them carnally** (Genesis 19:4-5).*

Thus the men of the city demanded that Lot turn over the men who had taken refuge under his roof. Why? *"That we may know them carnally,"* they shouted. This is *"going after strange flesh"* (Jude 7 KJV; see also Rom. 1:26-27). They weren't content to merely practice their sexual preferences privately. They lusted for more. Essentially, their evil intent was to abduct the two male travelers, abuse, violate, and forcefully rape them.

As in Noah's day, once again, to the moral Ruler of the Universe enough was enough. Unknown to that riotous crowd, it was Sodom's last night. Unexpectedly, the two travelers then stepped outside, raised holy hands, and—zap! Power flashed. The evil men were instantly blinded (see Gen. 19:10-11). A short time later, the two angels hurried Lot and his family out of that doomed city. In the wee hours of the morning:

The sun had risen upon the earth when Lot entered Zoar. Then the Lord rained brimstone and fire on

Sodom and Gomorrah, from the Lord out of the heavens. So He overthrew those cities, all the plain, all the inhabitants of the cities, and what grew on the ground (Genesis 19:23-25).

Significantly, in the barren sands on the edges of the Dead Sea, archeologists have discovered the ruins of ancient cities offering clear evidence that they were destroyed by fire. The ashes are there today. Bryant G. Wood, PhD, in his 2008 article published by the Associates for Biblical Research, wrote:

> When the archaeological, geographical and epigraphic evidence is reviewed in detail, it is clear that the infamous cities of Sodom and Gomorrah have now been found. What is more, this evidence demonstrates that the Bible provides an accurate eyewitness account of events that occurred southeast of the Dead Sea over 4,000 years ago.[12]

As with the destruction of Jerusalem in A.D. 70, biblical, archeological, and historical evidence for the literal destruction of Sodom and Gomorrah sounds another warning down the ages to our own day.

Let's be clear.

That warning is against *sexual immorality.*

And again—at the risk of being overly repetitious—I realize that sex sins aren't new. But again, just look around. Marriage is under fire like never before. Gender confusion is rampant, even among children. LGBTQ controversies keep rising. And on the World Wide Web, online pornography, "strange flesh" websites, escort services, and child sex trafficking are multiplying like rabbits.

Even the coronavirus pandemic boosted online porn because, due to stay-at-home orders, predators gleefully realized that millions of isolated potential victims were no longer at their workplaces but on their home computers. Truly, our world is experiencing an unprecedented deluge of sexual perversity.

Those who still believe in biblical values are aghast.

It's Sodom and Gomorrah, Part II.

In such an environment, this sober warning from Jesus Christ couldn't be more relevant: *"As it was in the days of Lot…so shall it be"* before His return. *"Escape for your life!"* urged holy angels, speaking to Lot (Gen. 19:17). Unseen, those same angels are speaking to us today.

The truth is, we *all* have struggles, temptations, and evil tendencies. Many of us wrestle with strong desires and feelings we don't want or don't know how to control. If this applies to you, don't give up. Rest assured that, no matter who you are or what you have sunk into, your Creator still loves you and wants to help you. *"Come to Me... learn from Me...and you will find rest for your souls"* is the tender appeal of our loving Savior (Matt. 11:28-29).

Jesus is big enough to handle our greatest problems. *"He is also able to save to the uttermost those who come to God through Him"* in sincere repentance and simple faith (Heb. 7:25). He is able to rescue us from bottomless pits and to piece our shattered lives back together that we may shine as trophies for His glory.

ANGRY NATIONS

Near the end of the eleventh chapter of the Book of Revelation sits this potent Bible verse:

The nations were angry, and Your wrath has come,
And the time of the dead, that they should be judged,
And that You should reward Your servants the prophets and the saints,
And those who fear Your name, small and great,
*And should **destroy those who destroy the earth*** (Revelation 11:18).

This unique passage lists this sequence of events:

1. Angry nations
2. The final arrival of God's just wrath in "the seven last plagues" (see Rev. 16)
3. The time of the dead, that they should be judged (see Rev. 20:11-13)
4. The time of rewards to be given to prophets and saints who fear God above man.
5. The time when God will finally "destroy those who destroy the earth."

My focus here will be point 1. In the final section of this chapter we will examine point 5.

John wrote: "The nations were angry."

According to the biblical record, the first angry person on earth after the entrance of sin was Cain, the first son of Adam and Eve. *"Cain was very angry"* because God didn't accept his sacrifice of fruit at His altar (Gen. 4:5). Instead, the Lord required a lamb—which pointed forward to the future supreme sacrifice of His only Son to redeem sinners from sin.

But Cain didn't like God's plan.

I'll worship my way, he decided.

His brother Abel was different. Acknowledging his sinfulness, and out of gratitude for his Creator's mercy, Abel *"brought the firstborn of his flock...And the Lord respected Abel and his offering"* (Gen. 4:4). A short time later, *"Cain rose up against Abel his brother and killed him"* (Gen. 4:8). This was the first murder that had ever occurred on earth.

The New Testament later reports:

*For this is the message that you heard from the beginning, that we should love one another, **not as Cain who was of the wicked one** and murdered his brother. And why did he murder him? Because his works were evil and his brother's righteous* (1 John 3:11-12).

Here John informs us that the hidden reason why Cain became so angry and finally killed his brother was because he *"was of the wicked one."* This means that Cain—most likely without realizing it—had become a child of the devil. This reveals a deep biblical truth. Whenever an individual stubbornly continues to forge his or her own way, rather than humbly submitting to God's perfect will and way, this by default places that person in the camp of the enemy.

"The wicked one" was the first rebel. Originally named *lucifer*, which means "light bearer," this mighty angel became proud, rebelled against his Maker, and deceived a third of God's holy angels to follow his dark path (see Isa. 14:12-14). Finally, *"war broke out in heaven"* (Rev. 12:7); but satan and his evil hosts suffered defeat. They were then kicked out of heaven and cast down to our earth (see Rev. 12:9). After leading Adam and Eve into sin, planet Earth became their headquarters.

According to biblical chronology, for approximately 6,000 years a fierce battle has been raging between good and evil, right and wrong, truth and error, obedience and disobedience, holy angels and fallen angels, between those who have chosen to follow in the footsteps of Abel and those who have *"gone in the way of Cain"* (Jude 11).

The last battle will soon be fought.

It's called Armageddon.

We will look more closely at that battle soon.

Revelation 12—the very chapter that describes the first war in heaven—carries us down to earth's sunset days, and gives us this warning:

*Woe to the inhabitants of the earth and the sea! For the devil has come down to you, **having great wrath**, because he knows that he has **a short time** (Revelation 12:12).*

This takes us down to earth's closing moments before the end of the world. The devil, we are told, has come down to the inhabitants of the earth and the sea with great wrath (fury), because he knows his time is running out fast. This is the underlying reason why *the nations were angry,* as pointed out in Revelation 11:18. Just like the wicked one inspired Cain to kill Abel, even so is he working invisibly behind the scenes to fuel anger, hatred, and rage among the nations in these last days.

Personally, I've been a Bible-believer for just over 40 years; but in all my days, I have never seen such hostility and hate between different groups, factions, political parties, races, and skin colors as we are witnessing today. Due to differences in theology, politics, and ideologies, it is often very difficult for two people with differing viewpoints to carry on a normal conversation and to just cordially agree to disagree. Respect, civility, and basic decency are fast disappearing and are being replaced by unreasoning rage, violence, riots, mayhem, and murder.

The spirit of Cain is rising.

Present-day Abels are in the minority.

"The nations were angry," predicted God's Word.

By His grace, let's avoid being infected by this raging pandemic.

GLOBAL ENVIRONMENTAL CRISIS

As we just discovered, the Bible reveals that when the Creator of all life finally drops the curtain on sinful, rebellious, devil-influenced, mixed-up, fallen human history, He will finally *"destroy those who **destroy the earth**"* (Rev. 11:18).

It is not my purpose here to discuss the ups, downs, ins, outs, and sideways controversies surrounding climate change, our dependence on fossil fuels, the effects of carbon dioxide, global warming, green legislation, and alternative sources of energy. Instead, I will highlight the biblical prediction—and ultimate solution (more on this soon)—that humans will be destroying the earth before King Jesus returns.

"In the beginning," when *"God created the heavens and the earth"* (Gen. 1:1), His Earth was exceedingly beautiful. *"In six days the Lord made the heavens and the earth, the sea, and all that is in them, and rested the seventh day"* (Exod. 20:11).

Have you ever wondered why we organize our entire lives around a seven-day week? It's not because of how long it takes for our earth to rotate completely on its axis, which marks off days. Or how long it takes for the moon to orbit the earth, which establishes our months. Or how long it takes for the earth itself to completely circle the sun, which is how we calculate years. Significantly, there is no planetary basis for a seven-day week.

So, where does it come from?

The simple answer is—from God. That's how our Creator set things up in the beginning, as recorded in Genesis 1 and 2.

As you can see, I'm not an evolutionist. I don't accept the Big Bang theory, which speculates that everything we see around us originated in a mindless, unorganized blast billions of years ago. The world itself, the mindboggling structure of cells with their complex DNA strands, and human brains are far too complicated to have sprung up by chance. As many credible scientists now realize, Charles Darwin was mistaken. His theory of natural selection has many flaws.[13]

Instead of speculative evolutionary theories, I accept the biblical account that a Master Designer formed our world in six days and rested on the seventh day (see Gen. 1; 2:1-3). The sacred record also states that when the King of the Universe gazed upon the fruit of His incomprehensible creative activity, He saw that *"indeed it was very good"* (Gen. 1:31). Everything was perfect! The original home of Adam and Eve was a *"garden"* in a lush region called *"Eden"* (Gen. 2:10). Unlike Babylonian, Persian, Greek, or Roman mythology, this is Bible truth.

Doesn't living in Paradise sound nice?

Try to imagine it. Unbelievably gorgeous trees. Luscious fruit. Colorful flowers. Crystal clear rivers and streams. Friendly animals. Fresh air. Bright mornings and pleasant evenings. The wonderful truth is that God created all of these things to make Adam and Eve happy. They were also free to eat from the tree of life (see Gen. 2:9), which grew *"in the midst of the Paradise of God"* (Rev. 2:7). The Bible says that *"God is love"* (1 John 4:8), and at the beginning of time, evidence for His love was everywhere.

Until sin messed everything up. Now, after thousands of years of human meandering, our formerly perfect planet is in a terrible state of crisis. Instead of living in the Garden of Eden, too many of us live in crowded cities. Rather than breathing life-giving fresh air, we inhale smog. Our forests are vanishing. Immense factories daily pump hazardous, cancer-causing pollutants into our environment. Our protective ozone layer is disintegrating. There's even one whole section in the Pacific Ocean between California and Hawaii nicknamed, "The Great Pacific Garbage Patch." It stinks. It's ghastly, being filled with plastic trash, chemical sludge, and other human debris flowing in from North and South America, and from as far as Asia.

Adam and Eve would probably faint if they saw it.

As much as we may try to become better stewards of our common home—which we *should* be—the truth is that there is no permanent earthly solution to our present environmental woes. The problem is too deep. It's systemic. Today, God speaks to us through His prophet, saying:

> *Lift up your eyes to the heavens, and look upon the earth beneath: for the heavens shall vanish away like smoke, and the earth shall wax old like a garment, and they that dwell therein shall die in like manner* (Isaiah 51:6 KJV).

In this time of the end, the very fabric of nature seems to be ripping apart at the seams. At an astonishing rate, earth's interconnected environmental systems are disintegrating. Left and right, deadly natural disasters strike. What's happening? God's Word gives the answer. After nearly 6,000 years of human sin, the earth is waxing *"old like a garment."* We seem to be on a collision course with self-annihilation.

If your house caught fire in the middle of the night while you were sleeping soundly, and you didn't know it, wouldn't you want one of your neighbors to sound a warning to wake you up? Similarly, it is time to try to wake up those in our world who are willing to listen and to tell them that we have reached an emergency.

Human lives are at stake.

Nearly 2,000 years ago, the book of Revelation predicted that this crisis would finally come upon us. After being patient, and then more patient, and then still even more patient watching what sinful humans have been doing to His once-perfect world, the Bible reports that the midnight hour will finally strike when God Himself will act justly to *"destroy those who destroy the earth"* (Rev. 11:18). Nevertheless, there's Good News, too. When the dust settles, our Magnificent Creator has promised, *"Behold, I make all things new"* (Rev. 21:5).

More about that soon.

Stick with me.

DECLINING MORALITY, EVEN AMONG PROFESSORS OF RELIGION

With so many biblically predicted signs clustering around us with each passing hour, one would think that countless believers in God would be even more careful to put away their sins, to seek the Lord, and to commit themselves to living pure, upright, unselfish lives and, by God's grace, to do their best to reveal His infinite love to a lost and dying world.

There is no doubt that many are committed to doing just that. They can be found in all churches and denominations, and even among sincere practitioners of non-Christian religions. But sadly, God's Word also predicts that a sizable group among the professedly religious will be doing just the opposite. As I focus on this dismal—yet plainly prophesied—trend, this will be the last sign highlighted in this chapter.

Notice carefully what Paul wrote:

*But know this, that **in the last days** perilous times will come: For men will be lovers of themselves, lovers of money, boasters, proud, blasphemers, disobedient to parents, unthankful, unholy, unloving, unforgiving, slanderers, without self-control, brutal, despisers of good, traitors, headstrong, haughty, lovers of pleasure rather than lovers of God, **having a form of godliness but denying its power**. And from such people turn away!* (2 Timothy 3:1-5)

Here the apostle Paul, looking forward to the last days of human history, wrote that perilous times would come. Surely the word *perilous* fits the times in which we live.

Then Paul penned a lengthy list of specific sins, evils, and offenses that would characterize those (these) days. Some of these sins refer to evil behaviors, such as those who are "blasphemers" (people who regularly speak blasphemous words against God), kids who are rudely disobedient to parents, and slanderers, which means those who unjustly make false statements about others.

So be careful what you post on social media!

Yet most of the sins Paul lists go much deeper than mere words or acts. Instead, they describe the inner condition of the heart, which could be compared to the underground roots of a tree that bears nasty or poisonous fruit. Such roots are that men (and women, too) will be lovers of themselves, lovers of money, boasters, proud, unloving, unholy, and unthankful.

Multitudes will be "without self-control," which implies that they just can't stop performing wicked deeds and have become slaves to harmful addictions, vice, and sin. Many are even brutal or cruel. Like Cain, they despise those who are good (like Abel). Apostatizing from their Creator, they become traitors to His government, His truth, His will, His Law, His Spirit, His grace, and His Word.

But it hardly bothers them. Regularly stifling the convictions of the Holy Spirit pricking their consciences, they become headstrong and haughty, just like the devil.

In a time when entertainment has become the virtual god of millions, multitudes have become lovers of pleasure rather than lovers of God. It's not wrong to want to feel good. We all want that. But these make pleasure, feelings, desires, lusts, and cravings all-important.

"If it feels good, do it!" becomes their motto.

But what is so shocking about Paul's list is the last part, recorded in verse 5. Surprisingly, the last part shows that Paul isn't primarily describing the world at large in the last days, but rather a condition among professors of spirituality. Look closely. Those guilty of such evils have *"a form of godliness,"* which means they perform the outward acts of religion, but they deny the power of God freely available to everyone to help us in this battle of life.

What is even more tragic is that many who profess religion and spirituality simply don't want to hear straight biblical truth. In the last chapter of that same book, Paul added:

> *For the time will come when they will not endure sound doctrine, but according to their own desires, because they have **itching ears**, they will heap up for themselves teachers; and **they will turn their ears away from the truth, and be turned aside to fables*** (2 Timothy 4:3-4).

Have you heard of *itching ears disease?* In these last days it's rampant—even more so than COVID-19. Unable to endure sound doctrine, those infected by it are constantly itching for smooth messages, pleasing fables, and soft sermons that require no one to turn from sin. But the reality is that real Bible truth sometimes hurts our pride; yet like good medicine that may taste terrible, we desperately need it.

Solid Bible truth is the best thing for us.

It can heal our souls.

Perhaps you've seen the TV commercial during which a hi-tech voice declares, "You have reached the end of the internet." Similarly, you have reached the end of this sobering chapter. If we are each brutally honest, none of us has wholly escaped Paul's last-days sin list. We are all sinners, and we too fight inner strongholds of evil within our own hearts.

But there is hope for us all, because there is a super-gracious God in heaven who loves us deeply and who longs to help us no matter who we are, what our situation is, or what kind of a stinking, rotten mess we've gotten ourselves into. As the famous hymn writer wrote:

> Amazing grace, how sweet the sound
>
> That saved a wretch like me.
>
> I once was lost, but now I'm found,

Was blind, but now I see!

It also won't be long until you reach the last chapter of *Approaching Armageddon*. It's called "Hope Beyond Darkness."

I pray it will give you hope, too.

NOTES

1. Shaena Montanari, "This Man Claims He Is Jesus Christ Reincarnated," NationalGeographic.com, July 12, 2017, https://www.nationalgeographic.com/photography/proof/2017/07/jesus-messiah-faith-social-media/?cmpid=org=ngp::mc=crm-email::src=ngp::cmp=editorial::add=SpecialEdition_Escape_20200723&rid=865677FF6300C169CEBE4B3AB955DC43.

2. Ibid.

3. "Who Is Pastor Apollo C. Quiboloy?" https://www.apolloquiboloy.com/who-is-pastor-apollo-quiboloy.

4. Ibid., https://www.apolloquiboloy.com/genuine-repentance.

5. Milton Leitenberg, "Deaths in Wars and Conflicts in the 20th Century, 3rd ed.," (Cornell University Peace Studies Program, August, 2006), https://www.clingendael.org/sites/default/files/pdfs/20060800_cdsp_occ_leitenberg.pdf.

6. H.J. Mai, "UN Warns Number of People Starving to Death Could Double Amid Pandemic," NPR, May 5, 2020, https://www.npr.org/sections/coronavirus-live-updates/2020/05/05/850470436/u-n-warns-number-of-people-starving-to-death-could-double-amid-pandemic.

7. Staff, "Outbreak: 10 of the Worst Pandemics in History," MPHonline.org, 2020, https://www.mphonline.org/worst-pandemics-in-history.

8. Ibid.

9. Mary Muscari, "Media violence: advice for parents," National Library of Medicine, December, 2002, https://pubmed.ncbi.nlm.nih.gov/12593343.

10. Gilda Sedgh et al., "Abortion Incidence between 1990 and 2014: Global, Regional, and Subregional Levels and Trends," *The Lancet* 388, no. 10041 (2016): pp. 258-267, https://doi.org/10.1016/s0140-6736(16)30380-4.

11. Ken Ham and Bodie Hodge, *A Flood of Evidence: 40 Reasons Noah and the Ark Still Matter* (Green Forest, AR: Master Books, 2016).

12. Bryant G. Wood, "The Discovery of the Sin Cities of Sodom and Gomorrah," Associates for Biblical Research, 1999, https://biblearchaeology.org/research/patriarchal-era/2364-the-discovery-of-the-sin-cities-of-sodom-and-gomorrah.

13. To learn more, read *Darwin's Black Box: The Biochemical Challenge to Evolution* by Michael J. Behe, Professor of Biological Science at Lehigh University. In the book summary, we read:

Naming *Darwin's Black Box* to the National Review's list of the 100 most important nonfiction works of the twentieth century, George Gilder wrote that it "overthrows Darwin at the end of the twentieth century in the same way that quantum theory overthrew Newton at the beginning." Discussing the book in *The New Yorker* in May 2005, H. Allen Orr said of Behe, "he is the most prominent of the small circle of scientists working on intelligent design, and his arguments are by far the best known." From one end of the spectrum to the other, *Darwin's Black Box* has established itself as the key text in the Intelligent Design movement—the one argument that must be addressed in order to determine whether Darwinian evolution is sufficient to explain life as we know it, or not.

CHAPTER 8

MASS ANIMAL DIE-OFFS

> "The innocence of childhood is like the innocence of a lot of animals."
>
> —Clint Eastwood, "What I've Learned"

> "Man is the only animal of which I am thoroughly and cravenly afraid."
>
> —George Bernard Shaw, Irish playwright

I've always liked animals. When I was a boy growing up in the Hollywood Hills, my family had cats, dogs, a bird, fish tanks, lizards, tadpoles, frogs, turtles, snakes, a chicken, rabbits, and a small alligator I named "Ali." After Kristin and I married, and when our children were little, we visited many zoos, such as the Los Angeles Zoo, the Sacramento Zoo, and the Portland Zoo.

At this moment, the Wohlberg family has two dogs (Pooka and Eva) and three cats (Princess, Prince, and Lacy). We also have six bird feeders outside our living room window. Deer and turkeys show up regularly in our backyard and sometimes even racoons. A young moose walked through our yard once. We also saw a wolf. During one of our family vacations, my daughter Abby was given the happy privilege of swimming with dolphins. She loved it!

Animals are awesome. The first book of the Bible plainly reveals where animals and birds originated:

Out of the ground the Lord God formed every beast of the field and every bird of the air, and brought them to Adam to see what he would call them. And whatever Adam called each living creature, that was its name. So Adam gave names to all cattle, to the birds of the air, and to every beast of the field (Genesis 2:19-20).

Surely Adam must have had a fantastic time naming all these fuzzy, furry, feathery, fascinating-looking creatures. It seems clear from these verses that animals were created to increase the happiness of humans. They were created to add more joy to our lives. They were to be our friends. As many of us know, strong emotional bonds can be formed between humans and horses, dogs, cats, and countless other creatures made by God. Although the entrance of sin has clouded our perceptions of God's original plan, yet even now we can still learn valuable lessons from His humble creatures. In the biblical book of Job 12, we read these words:

> But now ask the beasts, and they will teach you;
> And the birds of the air, and they will tell you;
> Or speak to the earth, and it will teach you;
> And the fish of the sea will explain to you.
> Who among all these does not know
> That the hand of the Lord has done this,
> In whose hand is the life of every living thing,
> And the breath of all mankind? (Job 12:7-10)

Here we are told that the beasts can teach us lessons, that the birds of the air can give us instruction, and that fish of the sea can explain to us many things—all without words.

It's also interesting to note that when ancient Israel drifted into gross sins, the effects of human wickedness spilled over to God's creatures, too. In Hosea 4, God's prophet first highlighted the terrible activities occurring among humans:

Hear the word of the Lord,

You children of Israel,

For the Lord brings a charge against the inhabitants of the land:

There is no truth or mercy

Or knowledge of God in the land.

By swearing and lying,

Killing and stealing and committing adultery,

They break all restraint,

With bloodshed upon bloodshed (Hosea 4:1-2).

This divinely inspired rebuke was called forth because, even among God's chosen people, horrific evils had become rampant. Truth, mercy, and knowledge of God had largely vanished. The Ten Commandments—which forbid swearing (third commandment), lying (ninth commandment), killing (sixth commandment), stealing (eighth commandment), and committing adultery (seventh commandment)—were publicly and regularly violated.

This sounds a lot like our world today, doesn't it?

In those ancient times, God faithfully warned His people that if they didn't repent, His just judgments would eventually fall on them:

And it shall be: like people, like priest.

So I will punish them for their ways,

And reward them for their deeds (Hosea 4:9).

Now here's an amazing detail embedded within this tragic narrative. The same chapter in the book of Hosea that warned about the evils of breaking God's holy Ten Commandment law also warned that as a consequence of human wickedness innocent animals would suffer, too. Notice carefully this shocking, prophetic passage:

Therefore [because of human wickedness described in verses 1 and 2] *the land will mourn;*

And everyone who dwells there will waste away

With the beasts of the field

And the birds of the air;

Even the fish of the sea will be taken away (Hosea 4:3).

Did you catch that? Because of human sin, and as a *sign of His pending judgment upon man,* the beasts of the field and the birds of the air would waste away. Even the fish of the sea would be taken away.

Fast-forward nearly 2,700 years from the time of Hosea to the time of the end. As part of the present signs of the times, we are now witnessing a most unusual, unprecedented, and often unexplainable phenomenon—*mass die-offs of animals, birds, fish, bats, bees, and insects.* The following is just a snapshot of news reports during only a four-year window of time (from 2011 to 2015):

- January 1, 2011: 5,000 blackbirds fell from the sky dead in Beebe, Arkansas.

- January 3, 2011: Approximately 2 million dead fish washed up in Chesapeake Bay.

- January 4, 2011: Approximately 500 birds fell out of the sky dead in Louisiana.

- January 7, 2011: Approximately 8,000 doves reigned down dead in Italy.

- February 16, 2011: An estimated 5 million fish washed up dead in the Mara River, Kenya.

- March 8, 2011: Millions of fish washed up dead in King Harbor Marina, California.

- May 13, 2011: Thousands of dead fish washed up on the shore of Lake Erie.

- July 15, 2011: Hundreds of thousands of prions (birds) found dead in New Zealand.

- August 1, 2011: Thousands of fish died in a lake that turned blood red in Texas.

- January 2, 2012: 20 tons of dead fish washed ashore in Norway.

- January 7, 2012: Thousands of dead fish found in the Gholani River, India.

- April 25, 2012: Porpoises died in alarming numbers near China.

- May 30, 2012: "Red tide" killed 55 million abalone in China.

- July 6, 2012: 60 million oysters dead, leaving farmers broke in Quang Ninh, Vietnam.

- November 12, 2012: Mass deaths of sea gulls turning beaches into mass graves in Morocco.

- December 31, 2012: 300 blackbirds dropped out of the sky dead in Tennessee.

- December 31, 2012: Thousands of tons of herring washed ashore dead in Iceland.

- January 11, 2013: Thousands of birds washed up dead on Michigan's shoreline.

- January 25, 2013: Millions of oysters wiped out in New South Wales, Australia.

- February 8, 2013: Immeasurable number of dead fish spanned 40 kilometers of the Fitzoy River, Australia.

- March 21, 2013: Millions of prawns washed up dead in Chile.

- April 8, 2013: Thousands of birds washed up dead in England.

- April 9, 2013: 190 Vultures dropped from the sky dead in Trinidad.

- July 12, 2013: Hundreds of thousands of dead eels covered beachfront in China.

- August 6, 2013: Hundreds of thousands of dead fish washed ashore in Pakistan.

- September 16, 2013: Crows and pigeons dropped from the sky dead in Nepal.

- January 26, 2014: 10 million scallops washed up dead in the waters near Vancouver, Canada.

- May 26, 2014: Hundreds of thousands of dead fish washed ashore in Texas.

- June 26, 2014: Thousands of dead sea birds found along the coast of Peru.

- August 26, 2014: Thousands of dead fish washed ashore in Saudi Arabia.

- September 22, 2014: Birds dropped out of the sky dead in Russia.

- December 18, 2014: 30 million dead fish washed up in a lake in Bolivia.

- January 15, 2015: Over 100,000 dead birds washed up on beaches in the U.S. and Canada.

Shockingly, these accounts represent only *a tiny fraction* of news reports from 2011 to 2015. If you do your homework, you will discover nearly 2,500 additional headlines covering many more mass animal die-offs during those same four years.

One of the most apocalyptic-sounding reports concerns the mysterious decimation of honeybee populations worldwide. Labeled "Colony Collapse Disorder" (CCD), the phenomena is "characterized by the sudden—overnight, in some cases—loss of the vast majority of the hive, leaving a queen, full brood (larvae) cells, and full honey stores behind." You can learn some basic facts on the website of the Planet Bee Foundation. It's lead article, "The Vanishing of the Bees," says this:

> Most recent evidence points to a combination of factors as the culprit—according to the USDA, these factors include "parasites and pests, pathogens, poor nutrition, and sublethal exposure to pesticides."[1]

What makes colony collapse disorder so potentially catastrophic is that fully "one-third of the food on our tables is there because of honeybees, which pollinate a wide array of the foods we love and need, and their survival is required to fuel both our bodies and our economy. Forget about berries, fruits, many vegetables if we fail to address this honeybee crisis."[2]

The front cover of the August 19, 2013 issue of *Time* magazine was entitled, "A World Without Bees: The Price We'll Pay If We Don't Figure Out What's Killing the Honeybee." The feature article, written by Bryan Walsh, declared:

> Honeybees "are the glue that holds our agricultural system together," wrote journalist Hannah Nordhaus in her 2011 book, *The Beekeeper's Lament.* And now that glue is failing...The loss of the honeybees would leave the planet poorer and hungrier, but what's really scary is the fear that bees may be a sign of what's to come, a symbol that something is deeply wrong with the world around us. "If we don't make some changes soon, we're going to see disaster," says Tom Theobald, a beekeeper in Colorado. "The bees are just the beginning."[3]

If the bee crisis isn't resolved, the global consequences will "bee" catastrophic.

Unfortunately, the 2011–2015 trend of mass animal die-offs hasn't gone away. Here are a few more recent reports.

THE TERRIFYING PHENOMENON THAT IS PUSHING SPECIES TOWARDS EXTINCTION (*THE GUARDIAN*, FEBRUARY 25, 2018)

Hundreds of millions of starfish off the west coast of America began to "melt" into white gloop.

...at least 45,000 flying foxes [bats] were killed on one hot day in south-east Queensland. Some colonies had more dead bodies than living bats. Their corpses were piled thick on the ground as the three species there—the black, little red and grey-headed—were hit.

...there were about 250,000 adults [saiga antelopes in Kazakhstan]...a year later, the mothers fell sick and began to drop dead. "It wasn't as if the disease started at one end and spread—there was no time for transmission of the pathogen from animal to animal. It was too quick…Within two or three days, everything was dying. By the end of the week, every single one was dead."[4]

MYSTERY IN WALES: HUNDREDS OF DEAD BIRDS FALL FROM THE SKY (DECEMBER 12, 2019)

From Arkansas to Australia, thousands of birds have been mysteriously falling from the sky to their death.

…It appears to be happening all over the world, too—Canada, Beebe, Arkansas, and Australia—and it's not specific to the kind of bird either.

Many believe that the birds have been poisoned, hit by an airplane, or were flying under the influence of some berries.

Perhaps the reason is something more profound. As of now the case remains unsolved.[5]

PLUMMETING INSECT NUMBERS "THREATEN COLLAPSE OF NATURE" (*THE GUARDIAN*, FEBRUARY 10, 2019)

The world's insects are hurtling down the path to extinction, threatening a "catastrophic collapse of nature's ecosystems", according to the first global scientific review.[6]

WHY DID ONE-QUARTER OF THE WORLD'S PIGS DIE IN A YEAR? (*THE NEW YORK TIMES*, JANUARY 1, 2020)

By the end of August 2019, the entire pig population of China had dropped by about 40 percent. China accounted for more than half of the global pig population in 2018, and the epidemic there alone has killed nearly one-quarter of all the world's pigs.[7]

Think of it. *Nearly a fourth of the world's pigs dead!* What on earth is going on? What's happening to all of these animals, birds, and insects? Theories abound, including climate change, heat, cold, diseases, pollution, pesticides, even airplanes. But in many cases, scientists just don't know for sure.

Rewind back to the days of Noah. It is interesting to note that just a few days before trillions of tons of water descended, God gave humanity one last sign of pending judgment. Do you remember what it was? It was *a sign of animals and birds* entering the ark, unaided by human hands.

Onlookers were struck with fear.

Could Noah be right? they wondered. Noah had been faithfully warning the world for 120 years that God would soon destroy the earth with an overwhelming flood, but few took him seriously. Even after this final sign—a sign involving animals—of pending doom, they still refused to believe. Instead, they kept clinging to "scientific explanations" why a flood was impossible, to calm their fears.

But in Noah's day, all "scientific explanations" eventually got wet—very wet.

Those who believed in them drowned.

As we've already seen, in the days of ancient Israel God also warned His people through His prophet Hosea that because of brazen human sinfulness, divine judgment was coming. As a sign foreshadowing future consequences, *"the beasts of the field and the birds of the air"* would suffer, and *"even the fish of the sea will be taken away"* (Hos. 4:3). In the New Testament, after rehearsing some of ancient Israel's history, Paul wrote:

Now all these things happened to them [Israelites] ***as examples, and they were written for our admonition, upon whom the ends of the ages have come*** (1 Corinthians 10:11).

One final thought. In that February 25, 2018 article published by *The Guardian* referenced previously about 250,000 antelopes mysteriously dropping dead, the reporter wrote that "there was *almost something biblical* about the scene of devastation."

Almost biblical?

Personally, I would delete the word *almost*.

NOTES

1. Emily Erickson, "The Vanishing of the Bees," Planet Bee Foundation, accessed August 7, 2020, https://www.planetbee.org/colony-collapse-disorder.

2. Liz Judge, "TIME Magazine Envisions a World Without Honeybees," Earth Justice, August 9, 2013, https://earthjustice.org/blog/2013-august/time-magazine-envisions-a-world-without-honeybees.

3. Bryan Walsh, "The Plight of the Honeybee," *TIME*, August 19, 2013, https://content.time.com/time/subscriber/article/0,33009,2149141,00.html.

4. David Derbyshire, "The terrifying phenomenon that is pushing species towards extinction," The Guardian, February 25, 2018, https://www.theguardian.com/environment/2018/feb/25/mass-mortality-events-animal-conservation-climate-change.

5. Scripps Media, Inc., "Mystery in Wales: Hundreds of dead birds fall from the sky," ABC Tuscon, December 12, 2019, https://www.kgun9.com/the-morning-blend/mystery-in-north-wales-hundreds-of-dead-birds-fall-from-the-sky.

6. Damian Carrington, "Plummeting insect numbers 'threaten collapse of nature,'" The Guardian, February 10, 2019, https://www.theguardian.com/environment/2019/feb/10/plummeting-insect-numbers-threaten-collapse-of-nature.

7. Yanzhong Huang, "Why Did One-Quarter of the World's Pigs Die in a Year?" The New York Times, January 1, 2020, https://www.nytimes.com/2020/01/01/opinion/china-swine-fever.html.

CHAPTER 9

THE BATTLE OF ARMAGEDDON

> "If we lose, all the other things just don't really matter."
>
> —Kirk Cousins, American football quarterback

At age 61, I'm doing my best to stay in shape. For years I've been a runner, and our present home in the forests of North Idaho is a perfect place for jogging due to the almost endless logging roads that wind throughout vast areas of wilderness near our house. One recent morning—during the time I was writing this book—I awoke early and decided to hit the trails. Rounding a corner in an isolated stretch of woods, I passed a pick-up truck parked on the side of the road. The front door was half-open, and a woman stood near the back of the truck smoking a cigarette.

"Good morning," I said as I slowly jogged past the truck. The woman hardly responded, but her man did. He apparently had been fast asleep sprawled out on the front seat. Jerking up suddenly, the guy muttered "Holy X&*!" (I won't repeat the second word). Quickly realizing I was simply a friendly jogger passing by, he smiled and said, "Good morning back to you!"

I kept going, and that was the end of our dialog.

But as I kept trudging along beneath towering pine trees, I kept thinking about what had just happened. That man's two words, "Holy X&*!" kept rolling around inside my head. The man was unconscious at first, but as he awoke out of sleep the very first word out of his mouth was "Holy." *That's a good word!* I thought to myself. But this was followed by a swear word—which isn't good. *Good and bad*, I thought as I kept jogging, *such is the drama that occurs within every soul.*

Ever since Adam and Eve sinned, human bodies have become fierce battlefields between the forces of good and evil, truth and error, right and wrong, light and darkness, God and satan. Throughout history this war has waged. In the days of Noah, God said, *"My Spirit shall not strive with man forever"* (Gen. 6:3). In other words, evil was approaching its limits, even in the sight of a patient, merciful God.

After 120 years of Noah's preaching and pleading, God's Spirit eventually stopped striving. The world had finally passed its point of no return, and the Lord finally delivered all who had resisted His promptings to the master they had persistently chosen—His enemy, the devil. Satan took over. At that point, there was no more conflict between good and evil inside those who had crossed that line, for His Holy Spirit was completely withdrawn.

The wicked had become incorrigible.

Soon the rain fell.

Personally, I don't think the human race as a whole has reached such a dismal state of corruption and wickedness as in the time of Noah. Thankfully, there is still a lot of goodness, honestly, respect, decency, and unselfish love in our world. But unfortunately, the trend is downward. *"But evil men and impostors will grow **worse and worse**, deceiving and being deceived"* wrote Paul (2 Tim. 3:13). Gross immorality, school shootings, child abductions, brutality, and senseless violence keep rising.

"How long, O Lord!" cried a voice in Revelation 6:10.

That *is* the question. How long? How long will a God of love allow sin, suffering, and tragedy to ravage and ruin

His world? How long will He endure the horrible scenes that daily rise before His face like billowing black pollution from factory smokestacks? How long will He allow such heartache, pain, and countless tears? Will He ever rise up from His royal throne and declare, "That's enough!" The biblical answer is yes, He will.

That Day will come sooner than we think.

It's called *Armageddon*.

The last book of the Bible declares:

And he gathered them together into a place called in the Hebrew tongue Armageddon (Revelation 16:16 KJV).

It is vital to realize that this is the only time the word *Armageddon* is used anywhere in the Bible. Speculative and dramatic Hollywood films have been produced about this word, and it appears on the covers of numerous books written by both secular and Christian authors alike. Reporters sometimes speak of it in news reports. Yet few understand what "Armageddon" is really about.

To make a correct interpretation, we must look at the context of Revelation's solitary use of that word, which includes the verses immediately before it and right after it. Notice carefully:

And I saw three unclean spirits like frogs coming out of the mouth of the dragon, out of the mouth of the beast, and out of the mouth of the false prophet. For they are spirits of demons, performing signs, which go out to the kings of the earth and of the whole world, to gather them to the battle of that great day of God Almighty. "Behold, I am coming as a thief. Blessed is he who watches, and keeps his garments, lest he walk naked and they see his shame." And they gathered them together to the place called in Hebrew, Armageddon (Revelation 16:13-16).

Upon careful analysis, we discover:

1. Unclean, froglike spirits emerge out of the mouths of the dragon, the beast, and the false prophet.

2. They are "spirits of demons, performing signs" that "go out to the kings [and their kingdoms] of the earth and the whole world."

3. Those "of the earth" and of "the whole world" are then gathered by these wicked spirits "to the battle of that great day of God Almighty."

4. Jesus Christ tells His people He is coming like a thief, so they must keep watching and hold on to their garments (His robe of righteousness, compare with Rev. 3:5; 7:9-14).

5. The entire world is then gathered to "Armageddon."

It is outside the scope of this book to cover details about the dragon, the beast, and the false prophet, which are all described in Revelation 13 (I do this in my other book, *End Time Delusions*). But it is clear from verses 13 and 14 that we are reading about the global forces of evil at the end of time. We can also see clearly that the evil spirits working through these forces go out *"to the kings of the earth and the whole world,"* which tells us that the entire world is involved. We can also see that the global forces of evil are then gathered for a final battle that will occur on that great day of God Almighty. Jesus Christ then inserts, *"Behold, I am coming like a thief."* That final battle, *which occurs in connection with His return,* is called "Armageddon."

Putting these pieces together, we discover that the world at large, which by this time has wholly yielded itself to satan and his demons, is gathered for a final battle against God Himself. As in Noah's day, by this time the Holy Spirit has been fully and completely withdrawn from the earth (but not from God's true people, see John 14:16-17). At this time, there are only two groups—those on God's side and those who have chosen His enemy (see Rev. 22:11-12). Then the Lord Jesus Christ will return to rescue His waiting, watching, loyal people.

The final battle engages.

Obviously, lucifer loses—big time.

The truth is that there is no literal location named *Armageddon* anywhere on planet Earth. You won't find it on any map. This mysterious word is actually a combination of two words: 1) *Ar*, which means "mountain," and 2) *mageddon*, which is reminiscent of the ancient *"Valley of Megiddo"* (2 Chron. 35:22). In the Old Testament, the Valley of Megiddo was a place of bloody battles and great slaughters. In fact, many scholars suggest the literal meaning of Megiddo is "slaughter" or "cut off." Thus, the mysterious combo-word, *Ar-mageddon*, could literally be translated "Mountain of Slaughter" upon which God's global enemies are cut off.

In Chapter Two of *Approaching Armageddon* we looked at King Nebuchadnezzar's mysterious dream in which he saw a mammoth humanlike statue representing the kingdoms of men. Do you remember what finally happened to that towering metal man? A gigantic stone that *"was cut out of the mountain without hands"* flew down from the sky and broke in pieces the entire image (see Dan. 2:44).

That stone symbolizes the return of Jesus Christ. He is the Rock of Ages. The fact that the stone was cut out of a mountain without hands shows that man's hands, human hands, are not able to permanently solve earth's woes. It's impossible. As hard as we try, humans can't solve the sin problem, nor can we wipe out the devil and his angels. Only God can do that. Only Jesus can *"break in pieces and consume"* all the dark sins and evils of this lost and dying world. Daniel then said that *"the stone that struck the image became a great mountain and filled the whole earth"* (Dan. 2:35).

The "great mountain" symbolizes the eternal kingdom of God, as it is written, *"the God of heaven will set up a kingdom which shall never be destroyed; and the kingdom shall not be left to other people; it shall break in pieces and consume all these kingdoms, and it shall stand forever"* (Dan. 2:44).

The new Testament counterpart to Daniel 2:44 is Revelation 16:13-16, which describes a global gathering of the kings of the earth and of the whole world for the final battle. These worldwide forces of satan compose his global kingdom. They will all be gathered to Armageddon—to the Mountain of Slaughter. Thus, the mysterious word *Armageddon* refers to a worldwide battle at which the devil's global kingdom (his proud *"destroying mountain,"* see Jeremiah 51:25) will finally reap its just reward. It will be totally shattered, slaughtered, broken in pieces, and consumed by the all-powerful armies of King Jesus who has finally returned to permanently establish God's everlasting kingdom, His great mountain, destined to fill the whole earth.

The very next verses after verse 16, where the word *Armageddon* occurs, clearly describe the global, catastrophic, and utter decimation of satan's worldwide forces. Read it for yourself:

> *And he gathered them together into a place called in the Hebrew tongue Armageddon. And the seventh angel poured out his vial into the air; and there came a great voice out of the temple of heaven, from the throne, saying, It is done. And there were voices, and thunders, and lightnings; and there was a great earthquake, such as was not since men were upon the earth, so mighty an earthquake, and so great. And the great city was divided into three parts, and the cities of the nations fell: and great Babylon came in remembrance before God, to give unto her the cup of the wine of the fierceness of his wrath. And every island fled away, and the mountains were not found* (Revelation 16:16-20 KJV).

A close reading of this section makes it very clear that the final, apocalyptic battle of Armageddon reaches far beyond the territory of the Middle East. As it is written, *"the cities of the nations fell...and every island fled away, and the mountains were not found."* The following parallel section describes the glorious return of King Jesus and the final slaughter of all the nations who have been duped by lucifer's lying legionnaires. Read it reverently with a humble heart:

> *Now I saw heaven opened, and behold, a white horse. And He who sat on him was called Faithful and True, and in righteousness He judges and makes war. His eyes were like a flame of fire, and on His head were many crowns. He had a name written that no one knew except Himself. He was clothed with a robe dipped in blood, and His name is called The Word of God. And the armies in heaven, clothed in fine linen, white and clean, followed Him on white horses. Now out of His mouth goes a sharp sword, that with it He should strike the nations. And He Himself will rule them with a rod of iron. He Himself treads the winepress of the fierceness and wrath of Almighty God. And He has on His robe and on His thigh a name written: KING OF KINGS AND LORD OF LORDS* (Revelation 19:11-16).

The Good News of Armageddon is that Jesus Christ Himself, who is depicted in Revelation's sacred imagery as a Rider on a white horse, will finally return to do battle with satan's global forces of sin. He is heaven's Hero. He is *"Faithful and True."* Remember, He never lies. No matter how strong wickedness may appear, when the Lord Jesus returns *"in righteousness He judges and make war."*

No evil can stand against Him.

He is *"clothed with a robe dipped in blood,"* which points to the precious blood He shed on Calvary to wash away sins and to make the characters of those who believe in Him pure and clean (see Rev. 1:5; 12:11; 19:8). But to those who have rejected Him and made a league with his rebellious foes, it won't be pretty.

Their blood will flow.

And He isn't coming alone. He will be joined by the armies of heaven—His loyal, royal angels. Together, they kicked satan and his rebel angels out of heaven long ago (see Rev. 12:7-9). That was lucifer's first big defeat. Jesus especially conquered satan and his hosts when He cried out, *"It is finished!"* as He hung upon the cross (see John 19:30; Rev. 12:10). That was satan's second, fatal loss.

Armageddon will be Part 3.

Lucifer and his demons have no chance.

With His *sharp sword*, symbolizing His Word, which slashes out of His mouth, Jesus will strike the nations that have persistently spurned His forgiveness, love, and grace and sold themselves to satan at a cheap price. It will be time for heaven's true Sovereign to take over. Above all presidents, rulers, and earthly monarchs, He is *"KING OF KINGS, AND LORD OF LORDS"* (Rev. 19:16).

Three verses later, John wrote:

*And I saw the beast, the kings of the earth, and their armies, gathered together **to make war against Him who sat on the horse** and against His army. Then the beast was captured, and with him the false prophet who worked signs in his presence...These two were cast alive into the lake of fire burning with brimstone* (Revelation 19:19-20).

A parallel verse says:

These [the beast and his global forces] *will make **war with the Lamb**, and the Lamb will overcome them, for He is Lord of lords and King of kings; and those who are with Him are called, chosen, and faithful* (Revelation 17:14).

Both of these Bible passages plainly describe a fierce war against the Lamb of God Himself. At Armageddon, King Jesus will defeat all satanic conspirators gathered against Him. At the same time, He will also deliver His people who have resolutely resisted all demonic influences and, by His grace, taken a firm stand on His side. Revelation 17:14 describes this last group of blood-bought, blood-washed, heart-transformed commandos as *"called, chosen, and faithful."* Revelation 14:12 also describes His humble, Spirit-filled, loyal ones: *"Here is the patience of the saints; here are those who keep the commandments of God and the faith of Jesus."*

On the morning of September 11, 2001, that fateful day in American history when Islamic terrorists high-jacked airplanes and flew them into the Twin Towers in New York City, a man named Steve Miller was inside the fully intact South Tower of the World Trade Center just minutes after the North Tower burst into flames.

As Mr. Miller and his associates quickly descended from the 80th floor, Miller paused on the 55th floor to use the men's room. It was shortly after 9:00 a.m. "Shall I phone my wife?" he pondered. Suddenly a voice echoed over the PA system: "Don't panic. The building is safe. Return to your offices." Mr. Miller then glanced sideways at the flaming building right next door and saw people jumping from windows a thousand feet above the ground.

Should he obey the voice of his conscience, which told him to get out now, or the official voice that told him not to panic but to remain in the building? Thankfully for him, he made the right choice. He made a bolt for the stairs just as the second hijacked airplane exploded into the South Tower just a few floors above him.

Reaching the bottom of the stairs, he quickly raced outside and hurried across the bridge toward Brooklyn. He finally glanced back, just in time to see the building he was inside only moments ago vanish in a cloud of smoke. Upon his arrival at home his teary-eyed wife collapsed into his outstretched arms. "Oh, my God," she cried, "I thought you were dead."

As we approach *"the battle of the great day of God Almighty"* (Rev. 16:14), rest assured that your loving heavenly Father, His Son Jesus Christ, the Holy Spirit, and billions of loyal angels definitely want you to live forever and not die. Yes, it's true that the details of Revelation 16:13-21 (the context of Armageddon) and Revelation 19:11-16 (describing Jesus Christ's return) are graphic. And yes, there will be a great, bloody slaughter. But as gory as these descriptions are, their bottom-line message is meant to encourage us. The Rider on the white horse—whose name is Faithful and True—will win. Evil will someday be completely crushed and terminated forever, and our great God, whose heart *"is love"* (1 John 4:8), will finally put an end to this age-long conflict with sin, error, darkness, pain, and death.

As Steve Miller—who just barely survived 9/11—ran into the arms of his dear wife, why not drop to your knees, confess your sins, and fall right now into loving arms of your merciful Savior, Jesus Christ, the supreme Lover of your soul?

Humble yourselves in the sight of the Lord, and He will lift you up (James 4:10).

*The eternal God is thy refuge, and **underneath are the everlasting arms*** (Deuteronomy 33:27 KJV).

The one who comes to Me [Jesus] ***I will by no means cast out*** (John 6:37).

The choice is yours.

In the last chapter of *Approaching Armageddon* we'll take a closer look at God's love and at His incredible future, which He has planned for all who renounce the ruler of Darkness and instead choose the Prince of Life.

CHAPTER 10

HOPE BEYOND DARKNESS

> "We have always held to the hope, the belief,
> the conviction that there is a better life, a
> better world, beyond the horizon."
>
> —Franklin D. Roosevelt (1882-1945)
> 32nd President of the United States

I remember the month of July 2004 like it was yesterday. That was the month that our first child, Seth Michael Wohlberg, came into the world. Shortly before his birth, I was conducting a seminar before a large audience in scenic Soquel, California. One of my talks was entitled, "7 Years of Tribulation?" After speaking for about 30 minutes, the television monitors at the base of the platform I was standing on unexpectedly flashed:

LABOR NOW! LABOR NOW! LABOR NOW!

"Er...ah..." I stumbled. "I...I...I've got to go. My wife is having our baby!" Some friends quickly helped me gather my things, and I was soon driving down California State Highway 1 for a two-hour trip to a hospital in Templeton. Just to clarify: I knew my wife Kristin was at that hospital, but we both thought it was simply for a routine check-up. Seth wasn't due until August. But, as everyone knows, life doesn't always unfold as planned. After being examined by a nurse, and after running some tests, the physician in charge decided it was time for Seth to make his debut.

Kristin and I slept at the hospital that night. The next day, after Kristin was prepped, I also was admitted into the delivery room to join her for that special moment. After some initial instruction, Dr. Thomas told us it was time. "One, two, three, push!" he told his attendants. I'll never forget (in this life) what happened next. A few seconds later, out popped Seth like a flying missile, bloody and screaming wildly. Dr. Thomas gently picked up our son and placed him on a small cushioned table right next to me.

"Seth, Seth, it's your daddy!" were my exact words to him as he lay beside me screaming.

Suddenly, the most amazing thing happened. Seth's tiny mouth closed and he became silent. Then his two little eyes began darting back and forth. He was searching *for me*, his dad, because he recognized his father's voice.

When I was a boy growing up in the Hollywood Hills, I watched a movie called *The Grinch Who Stole Christmas*. At the end of the movie, the Grinch's heart enlarged three times, and he became a different person. Something like that happened to me when Seth became silent and searched for me. Suddenly, my heart enlarged, and I was changed. The love that I felt for Seth was indescribable—and it has continued to this day. Three years later Seth's little sister Abby arrived. Oh, how Kristin and I love our little girl! We love both of our children with a love that is beyond words.

Becoming a father has done something else to me. It has given me a deeper glimpse into the infinite love of God for me personally, for my family, and for all the rest of us. In this final chapter of *Approaching Armageddon*, I want to focus on God's love and on His plan for our future. Make no mistake about it—the revelation of His love is a central part of end-time Bible prophecy.

The last sign that Jesus listed in Matthew 24 is found in verse 14.

And this gospel of the kingdom will be preached in all the world as a witness to all the nations, and then the end will come (Matthew 24:14).

There is more to this verse than meets the eye at first glance. Let's unpack it. The word *gospel* means "Good News," which reveals the essence of the character of God. At His core, He is good—kind, unselfish, just, and merciful. It is so wonderful to discover that we are not here by chance and that our Creator is a supremely loving Being. *"God is love"* (1 John 4:8), reveals His Word. *"God is light and in Him is no darkness at all"* (1 John 1:5).

When Adam and Eve sinned, God's challenge was to extend His mercy and yet to maintain His justice at the same time. He can't overlook sin. In the counsels of heaven, a royal solution was agreed upon—one that both redeemed men and unfallen angels will be pondering throughout the ceaseless ages of eternity. Motivated by infinite love, the Father covenanted to sacrifice His Son on a cruel cross bearing *"the sin of the world"* (John 1:29).

Jesus fully agreed with this royal plan. He would suffer intensely, bearing the wrath of divine justice, in order to fully pay the price of human sin, which is the violation of the Ten Commandments, His law of love (see Exod. 20:1-20; 1 John 3:4; Rom. 3:20; 7:7,12; 13:10). *"Christ died for our sins"* is the essence of the gospel or Good News (1 Cor. 15:3).

Then He rose from the dead!

Now that I have become a father to Seth and Abby, I have become even more amazed at the depth of that love. Would I offer my own son for sinners? Or my daughter? I'm shaking my head as I write this. This would be very, very, very hard. I'm not sure I could ever do it. But God did. He sacrificed His Son for you and for me. You can search the world's religions—Islam, Buddhism, Hinduism, Wicca, etc.—but there is no religion on earth that has at its core such a divine sacrifice of love.

None.

Not one.

In Matthew 24:14, Jesus said that one of the final signs before Armageddon will be that His gospel, or Good News, will be preached to all the world. Stop for a moment and think about this prediction. When Jesus first said this, He was a humble carpenter-turned-preacher sitting on the Mount of Olives in the Middle East with a small band of devoted followers. From a human perspective, it seemed impossible that His message—His gospel—would someday belt the world.

What are the odds of that?

I'm not a gambling man; but if I was, those odds (humanly speaking) didn't look good. Again, think about it. If a new religious teacher were to rise up today and make such a claim, he would probably be viewed as a candidate for a mental institution. Who really is Jesus Christ? Humans have wrestled with this for two thousand years. "He was a good man," some say today. But this can't be right. Responses to the Prophecy Man can't be so neutral. He not only affirmed to His enemies that He was the Son of God, but that they would someday behold Him *"sitting at the right hand of the Power, and coming on the clouds of heaven"* (Matt. 26:63-64).

Jesus Christ was either a liar, a lunatic, or Lord of all.

He said His gospel would spread to all the world. Two thousand years later, because of the dedication of His true followers, and with the help of technology in "the time of the end," Christ's prophecy is being fulfilled before our eyes. With the aid of radio, television, satellites, the internet, YouTube, Facebook, podcasts, smartphones, Bible apps, etc., the Bible message of salvation through the death of Jesus Christ on a cruel cross for the sins of the whole world (see 1 John 2:2) is now being proclaimed all over planet Earth—even in remote villages in the Amazon jungle and in countless other places.

At White Horse Media (where I work), we've even heard lots of stories of men in shiny white garments appearing to tribal chiefs and jungle bandits, explaining the gospel or telling them to read the Bible. Many Muslims are having dreams and visions. We heard one story of a Muslim man who dreamed of the glory of Jesus, the Son of God. As he cautiously shared his dream with his Muslim friends, he discovered that everyone in his village had had *the same dream.* The entire village switched to believing in Jesus! Such stories could be multiplied.

It's an incontrovertible fact. Through missionaries, technology, and with the aid of holy angels, God's unstoppable "Good News" is advancing like never before. Someday soon—none know how soon—His work will be finished. Jesus said, *"then the end will come."* King Jesus will return *"on the clouds of heaven with power and great glory"* (Matt. 24:30).

The battle of Armageddon will be fought. Satan, his wicked angels, and all the hosts of lost humans who have chosen the dark ways of sin above repentance and sincere faith in Jesus Christ will be defeated at *"the battle of that great day of God Almighty"* (Rev. 16:14). Having rejected the Good News, they will tragically reap Bad News in *"the lake of fire. This is the second death. And anyone not found written in the Book of Life was cast into the lake of fire"* (Rev. 20:14-15).

The lake of fire is described in the last two verses of Revelation 20. Like a dramatic movie, immediately after those fiery verses there is a major scene change. I'm so glad for this. The Holy Bible teaches that the lake of fire is not the Last Act. No, no. The very next verses reveal:

Now I saw a new heaven and a new earth, for the first heaven and the first earth had passed away. Also there was no more sea. Then I, John, saw the holy city, New Jerusalem, coming down out of heaven from God, prepared as a bride adorned for her husband. And I heard a loud voice from heaven saying, "Behold, the tabernacle of God is with men, and He will dwell with them, and they shall be His people. God Himself will be with them and be their God. And God will wipe away every tear from their eyes; there shall be no more death, nor sorrow, nor crying. There shall be no more pain, for the former things have passed away." Then He who sat on the throne said, "Behold, I make all things new." And He said to me, "Write, for these words are true and faithful" (Revelation 21:1-5).

Try to imagine it. A new heaven and a new earth! Just like the Garden of Eden! And seated upon this beautiful, fresh, clean, purified-from-sin planet, our new capital will be *"the holy city, New Jerusalem,"* where God Himself and His people will live. And *"there shall be no more death, nor sorrow, nor crying. There shall be no more pain, for the former things have passed away."*

Think of all the awful signs that have been described in this book. Yet on God's bright new earth, everything bad will be gone. There will be no more:

- False prophets or false messiahs
- Bloody revolutions, conflicts, wars
- Earthquakes, storms, floods, fires
- Love growing cold
- Violence as in Noah's day
- Sexual immorality like Lot's day
- Global environmental crises
- Pollution, sludge, nuclear waste
- Anger among nations
- Heart disease, cancer, diabetes, COVID-19
- Gangs, riots, murders, drive-by shootings
- Heartache, stress, confusion
- Mass animal die-offs
- Funerals, cemeteries, tombstones

Death itself will disappear.

For the former things have passed away!

Will this really happen? John wrote: *"Then He who sat on the throne said, 'Behold, I make all things new.' And He said to me, 'Write, for these words are true and faithful'"* (Rev. 21:5). These words are the words of God. They *"are true and faithful,"* said a holy angel. When King Jesus descends on *"a white horse"* at Armageddon, He is called

"Faithful and True" (Rev. 19:11). Near the end of the Bible, His words are also true and faithful.

We can trust the Prophecy Man.

What the Old Testament predicted about the birth, life, and death of Jesus Christ was perfectly *fulfilled.*

After King Nebuchadnezzar had his mysterious dream, God's explanation given to His prophet Daniel about the rise and fall of nations has been, and is being *fulfilled.*

What Jesus predicted about the destruction of Jerusalem and the Jewish temple was *fulfilled* in A.D. 70.

The book of Daniel's prediction that in the time of the end knowledge would increase *is happening now.*

All of the signs that Jesus and other Bible writers said would occur *are also being fulfilled.*

Revelation's predictions that King Jesus will return and win the battle against evil at Armageddon *will soon be fulfilled.*

Even so will His promise to create a new heaven and a new earth and to utterly abolish all sickness, sorrow, pain, and death *also be fulfilled.*

We can trust the Word of God!

The last chapter of the Holy Bible ends with these words:

THE TIME IS NEAR

Then he said to me, "These words are faithful and true." And the Lord God of the holy prophets sent His angel to show His servants the things which must shortly take place.

"Behold, I am coming quickly! Blessed is he who keeps the words of the prophecy of this book."

Now I, John, saw and heard these things. And when I heard and saw, I fell down to worship before the feet of the angel who showed me these things.

Then he said to me, "See that you do not do that. For I am your fellow servant, and of your brethren the prophets, and of those who keep the words of this book. Worship God." And he said to me, "Do not seal the words of the prophecy of this book, for the time is at hand. He who is unjust, let him be unjust still; he who is filthy, let him be filthy still; he who is righteous, let him be righteous still; he who is holy, let him be holy still."

JESUS TESTIFIES TO THE CHURCHES

"And behold, I am coming quickly, and My reward is with Me, to give to every one according to his work. I

am the Alpha and the Omega, the Beginning and the End, the First and the Last."

Blessed are those who do His commandments, that they may have the right to the tree of life, and may enter through the gates into the city. But outside are dogs and sorcerers and sexually immoral and murderers and idolaters, and whoever loves and practices a lie.

"I, Jesus, have sent My angel to testify to you these things in the churches. I am the Root and the Off-spring of David, the Bright and Morning Star."

And the Spirit and the bride say, "Come!" And let him who hears say, "Come!" And let him who thirsts come. Whoever desires, let him take the water of life freely.

A WARNING

For I testify to everyone who hears the words of the prophecy of this book: If anyone adds to these things, God will add to him the plagues that are written in this book; and if anyone takes away from the words of the book of this prophecy, God shall take away his part from the Book of Life, from the holy city, and from the things which are written in this book.

I AM COMING QUICKLY

He who testifies to these things says, "Surely I am coming quickly." Amen. Even so, come, Lord Jesus! The grace of our Lord Jesus Christ be with you all. Amen (Revelation 22:6-21).

I am so thankful that the very last sentence in God's Book ends with the message that *the grace* of our Lord Jesus Christ is available to us *all*. This notifies us that abundant grace (which means *unmerited favor* we don't deserve) is now available to every one of us. Even me. Even you.

In our battles with sin, self, and satan, it's easy to get discouraged. In fact, there have been a number of times in my Christian journey that I was so utterly downcast that I thought there was no hope for me. "You're too sinful!" wicked spirits whispered maliciously. "Perhaps God loves others, but not you!" Believe me, I have battled such thoughts. Yet each time, when I thought I was sinking in quicksand never to rise again, the Lord encouraged me with promises like these:

*Look at the birds of the air, for they neither sow nor reap nor gather into barns; yet your heavenly Father feeds them. **Are you not of more value than they?*** (Matthew 6:26)

*For He Himself has said, "I will **never** leave you nor forsake you"* (Hebrews 13:5).

For I, the Lord your God, will hold your right hand, saying to you, "Fear not, I will help you" (Isaiah 41:13).

The Lord has appeared of old to me, saying: "Yes, I have loved you with an everlasting love; therefore with lovingkindness I have drawn you" (Jeremiah 31:3).

If we confess our sins, He is faithful and just to forgive us our sins and to cleanse us from all unrighteousness (1 John 1:9).

Be of good courage, and He shall strengthen your heart, all you who hope in the Lord (Psalm 31:24).

He has not dealt with us according to our sins, nor punished us according to our iniquities. For as the heavens are high above the earth, so great is His mercy toward those who fear Him; as far as the east is from the west, so far has He removed our transgressions from us. As a father pities his children, so the Lord pities those who fear Him. For He knows our frame; He remembers that we are dust (Psalm 103:10-14).

Rest in the Lord, and wait patiently for Him (Psalm 37:7).

None of those who trust in Him shall be condemned (Psalm 34:22).

Remember, when Seth first exited Kristin's body, he was crying uncontrollably. Then I said, "Seth, Seth, it's your daddy!" He stopped crying immediately. Why? Because He recognized his father's voice.

I sincerely hope and pray that you have heard your heavenly Father's voice in the pages of this book. Yes, I love Seth, Abby, and Kristin so much. But God loves each us much more. Don't let the devil convince you otherwise. He's a liar! If you ever wonder about Jesus Christ's love and whether there is hope for you, look at His cross. Behold His suffering, His pain, His agony, and even His separation from His own eternal Father because He was bearing the total load of our sins and guilt. This finally prompted His incomprehensible cry, *"My God, My God, why have You forsaken Me?"* (Matt. 27:46).

Dear reader, Jesus experienced all this—*just for you.*

If we forsake our sins and trust in His worthiness and in His Word, He is able to make us more than conquerors in these perilous last days that are now rapidly *Approaching Armageddon* (see Rom. 8:37; 2 Tim. 3:1).

His promise is: *"I am with you always, **even unto the end of the world"*** (Matt. 28:20 KJV).

I hope to see you on the other side of earth's final battle and to meet you on that peaceful shore.

ABOUT STEVE WOHLBERG

Steve Wohlberg is the speaker/director of White Horse Media. He is the author of 30-plus books, has been featured in three History Channel documentaries (*Secrets of the Seven Seals*; *Strange Rituals: Apocalypse*; *Armageddon Battle Plan*), and one National Geographic International documentary (*Animal Armageddon*) offering insights into the book of Revelation. He has also spoken by special invitation inside the Pentagon and U.S. Senate. He lives with his wife Kristin and their two children (Seth and Abby) in North Idaho. His passion is to be a good husband and father and to help others prepare for the return of Jesus. He enjoys gardening and the great outdoors.

MORE ENLIGHTENING BOOKS

BY STEVE WOHLBERG NOW AVAILABLE FROM
DESTINY IMAGE PUBLISHERS AND WHITE HORSE MEDIA

End Time Delusions:
The Rapture, the Antichrist, Israel,
and the End of the World

Demons in Disguise:
The Dangers of Talking to the Dead

End Times Health War:
How to Outwit Deadly Diseases
Through Super Nutrition and Following
God's 8 Laws of Health

DESTINY IMAGE PUBLISHERS, INC.

P.O. Box 310
Shippensburg, PA 17257-0310
1-800-722-6774

White Horse Media
P.O. Box 130
Priest River, Idaho 83856
1-800-782-4253
www.whitehorsemedia.com

STEVE WOHLBERG
VIDEO COURSES

AVAILABLE AT DESTINYIMAGE.TV:

Approaching Armageddon Master Class

Sprouting With Steve
(health course, learn to grow super healthy sprouts
and micro greens in your own home)

TV SERIES FROM WHITE HORSE MEDIA

(AVAILABLE ON DVD)

God: Fact or Fiction? Weighing the Evidence

*The Abortion Controversy: Two Women
Tell Their Stories of Hope and Healing*

*Coming Out: Former Gays Testify
of God's Saving Love*

Finding Hope in Depression and Despair

Is Jesus Kosher for Jews?

SIGN UP FOR STEVE WOHLBERG'S

free e-newsletter at
www.whitehorsemedia.com

Follow him on Twitter:
@WhiteHorse7

Find him on Facebook:
www.facebook.com/stevewohlberg